HUMAN ECOLOGY FOR GLOBALIZATION

BIODIVERSITY AND FOOD SECURITY

SHASHI KUMAR

ATLANTIC

ATLANTIC PUBLISHERS AND DISTRIBUTORS

Published by
ATLANTIC PUBLISHERS AND DISTRIBUTORS
B-2, Vishal Enclave, Opp. Rajouri Garden, New Delhi-27
Phones : 5413460, 5429987, 5466842

Sales Office
4215/1, Ansari Road, Darya Ganj, New Delhi-110 002
Phones : 3273880, 3285873, 3280451
Fax : 91-11-3285873
web : www.atlanticbooks.com
e-mail : info@atlanticbooks.com

ISBN 81-269-0125-X

Typeset at
APD Computer Graphics, Delhi

Printed in India at
Nice Printing Press, Delhi

PREFACE

The World is confronted today with the problem of poverty, hunger, ill-health and illiteracy on one hand, and continuing deterioration of the environment as the life support system of human beings on the other. The hope for a better and safe future for mankind lies in the integration of environment and development concern, which necessarily requires global co-operation.

Many ancient cultures had laid great emphasis on human-environment relationship and the modern industrialized cultures. We have to learn a lot from the scriptures such as the *Vedas* of *Aryan* culture in order to master the needed human-environment harmony.

The words 'ecology' and 'economy' stem from the same Greek root '*Oikos*' meaning 'house.' 'Economy' is the management of the house and 'ecology' is the study of the house and the house is the earth. Ecology is the study of the interactions between organisms and their environment. There are two distinct components of the environment : the physical environment (comprising temperature, water availability, wind speed, soil acidity) and biotic environment, which comprises influences on an organism that are exerted by other organisms including competition, predation, parasitism and co-operation.

Human ecology is the study of interactions between human beings and their environment. It is a means to improve people's lives and environment with the focus on interactions of humans reciprocal effects that take place physically, socially, economically and aesthetically.

The philosophy of human ecology provides the context for developing and serving the individuals and their families a productive quality of life. To take advantage of growing opportunity, matching human resources have to be developed. In view of rapid technological advancement, information explosion, diverse conditions and growing capabilities have made it imperative to develop HRD skills. Further, increasing the agricultural production for development in isolation is not the only issue but we have to address the issues of sustainability, environment and ecological imbalance, depleting natural resources and widening of regional and socio-economic inequity and thus have to maintain the biodiversity.

Ecology can be considered a scale from holistic system perspective moving from an individual's molecule to the entire global ecosystem. However, four identifiable subdivisions of scale of particular interest are : (i) individuals, (ii) populations, (iii) communities and (iv) ecosystems.

The term ecology and ecological roots were not expressed. During this time preservation of the environment and conservation of resources such as fossil fuel and water became matter of international concern. Action that threatened survival of various species of plants and animals created renewed interest in ecology, the science concerned with inter-relationships between organisms and the environment — both organic and inorganic.

The term ecosystem came into use and ecological roots of home science were rediscovered and taken as *Oekology*, the science which teaches the principles of healthy life. The term provided a philosophical basis for much of subsequent work in human ecology as it is applied to the family and to the home economics.

Human ecology attempts to break the barrier between rational scientific thought and the dogmatic beliefs of our ancient mythology. The wisdom contained in the ancient mythology is not only to be explained in layman's language, but also correlated to modern scientific principles. In fact science and mythology are not two different mutually exclusive disciplines of learning but merely two different languages of describing the same reality. After all human brain is the common hardware with the common reflexes, institutions, inspirations and aspirations. The glare of modern technology is constantly pushing back in our old knowledge and philosophy till we may forget it all together.

This is a serious threat to our ancient wisdom, a threat to the extent of its total elimination, a threat which may cause the complete loss of this magnificent heritage of our traditions and culture. Yet there is hope.

For, when the glare of technology overtakes moral values the society is trapped in conflicts. Conflicts between intellect and personalities; conflicts between morality and convenience. Then one is forced to revert to the scriptures. Peace of mind is ultimately found in the scriptures and not in technology.

There was a wealth of wisdom, lying hidden in our mythology which could stand the test of scientific scrutiny. Science has not divorced from our ancient wisdom. Fortunately, the latest knowledge in the field of computers and telecommunication makes it much easier to bridge the gap.

SHASHI KUMAR

CONTENTS

Preface vii

1. Concept of Human Ecology 1

2. Biodiversity Conservation and Sustainable Agriculture 14

3. Diverse Women for Diversity 28

4. Globalization of Food Insecurity 42

5. Globalization of Agriculture 53

6. Biological and Intellectual Heritage Protection 84

7. Status of Plant Genetic Resources Conservation and Utilization in Asia-Pacific Region 108

8. Ecology and Technological Changes 145

9. Gender and Society in India 172

10. Status of India's Health and Healing 219

Index 231

1
Concept of Human Ecology

R.S. PARODA*

HUMAN ECOLOGY, is the study of interactions between human beings and their environment. There are two distinct components to the 'environment' : the physical environment (comprising of temperature, water availability, wind speed, soil acidity) and biotic environment, which comprises influences on an organism that are exerted by other organisms, including competition, predation, parasitism and cooperation. It is a means to improve people's lives and environment with the focus on interactions of humans with their environment, emphasizing in depth study of reciprocal effects that take place physically, socially, economically and aesthetically.

In view of rapid technological advancement, information explosion, diverse conditions and growing capabilities has made it imperative to develop HRD skills of people for development. Further increasing the agricultural production for development in isolation is not the only issue but we have to address the issues of sustainability, environment and ecological imbalance, depleting natural resources and widening of regional and socio-economic inequity and have to maintain the bio-diversity.

In the last century the developments in science have led to unprecedented development and destruction. However, on a balance sheet we find that science has made our lives more livable. Scientific developments have resulted in controlling the menace of hunger, disease and poverty to large extent though the

* Director General, ICAR, New Delhi.

fight is still on and will continue so long as the human population continues to rise. Unfortunately, the rise in human population is more in countries/regions where we have more poverty. South Asia and sub-Saharan African regions are glaring examples of population and poverty nexus. It is here that the problem of environment/ecological degradation has manifested itself more than any other region. We in India have entered the new millenium with a much better report of socio-economic indicators *i.e.*, production of food grain 209 mt, 76 million tonnes of milk, 33 billion eggs, 40 mt of fruits, 87 million tonnes of vegetable etc. The per capita availability of essential items has also increased and today our per capita calorie intake is close to the recommended norm of 2300 cal./day required for a healthy and productive life. The average life expectancy has also increased from under 40 years around independence to 62 years now. Similarly, the literacy rates have gone up and child mortality rate has also declined.

In the new millenium India is well equipped, for its bio-industrial development. The scientific expertise, infrastructural facilities and research need to be strengthened by bonding the relationship between research and educational institutions and industry in a symbiotic mode of conversion of research findings into products, processes and technologies for human resource development.

People

The Green Revolution has won a temporary success in man's war against hunger, which if fully implemented, could provide sufficient food for mankind by the end of the 20th century. But unless the frightening power of human reproduction is checked the success of the Green Revolution would remain ephemeral. We have entered the 21st century, with a population of over one billion, that is about 16 per cent of the global population living on 2.6% of the global land.

Our experience in population management reveals that a target group oriented approach towards the poor, backward, uneducated, resourceless and especially the women is most effective. Improvement in literacy, in general, and female literacy, in particular, should receive our highest priority. There is wide disparity in the literate population in different states. For instance, there is 90 per cent literacy in Kerala compared to only 39 per cent in Rajasthan. The gender difference in literacy is also quite appalling. While 86 per cent females are literate in Kerala, it is only 21 per cent in Rajasthan. Further, policy initiatives like changing property rights in favour of women, increasing the number of women extension workers, strengthening the thrift initiatives by women and decision-making in agriculture have proved very helpful. Also the public health services and family welfare programmes in rural areas have helped. Population management is, therefore, most critical, or otherwise any effort made on the production front will always be thwarted by the population growth.

On account of very large and constantly expanding population base of the country, impact of efforts made on population control has been minimal. We may have to intensify these efforts made on population control has been minimal. We may have to intensify these efforts uniformly across all segments of the society. For wider acceptance and adoption of population control measures, mass awareness through media coupled with easy access and availability of population control devices should be ensured.

We should also envision that every child born in India has a right of food, nutrition and healthy life. Traditional foods and crops, which are nutritious and eco-friendly, need to be promoted. We may also look for alternative foods and also improve their quality to address protein-energy-malnutrition problem. Organic food production, modern food blended with traditional ones and developing designer crops/products should receive our attention.

Fortunately, ours is largely a vegetarian society and thus dependence on meat as a source of protein is much less as compared to other nations. Hence, our food feed competition will always be moderate. Besides several pulses that we grow, soyabean is now a natural choice for protein supplementation. Fighting hidden hunger and micronutrient deficiencies through fortification, supplementation, diversifying diets linked with changing food habits, breeding for designer crops such as golden rice or high quality protein maize (QPM) should receive greater attention. The recommendations of the World Nutrition Congress regarding political commitment, community mobilization and participation, human resource development, improving food distribution and storage, improving food processing and safety, and effective management of information systems need to be addressed as a national priority.

While being one of the two most populous countries of the world could be a curse, brighter side of it should be also seen. It is the people who are the most valuable asset of any nation and it is this power which determines our strength. Concurrent with the policy of population management, we must bring in policies that channelise our vast human resource into an enlightened society and make them responsible citizens committed towards national economic development. Towards nation building, we must generate enough work for the people while improving their power. The very strength of this power must be recognized and harnessed in our national interest.

Productivity

As agriculture seeks to be more productive and sustainable, it will need to be even more science-based than ever before to alleviate poverty. Often it is argued that our crop productivity and input use efficiency are quite low as compared to those of the developed countries. Obviously, I see this as an uncommon opportunity to improve productivity through effective integration and application of new science in various products, processes and services. Further, the comparative advantage of our products be based on uniqueness, differentiation and technology content. Intellectual capital and the technologies already generated are also to be effectively harnessed.

In a competitive environment, emphasis has to be put on efficient production systems. Coverage under high-yielding varieties will have to be further increased. Hybrid technology oriented policy, particularly under rainfed farming, needs promotion. India has already demonstrated world leadership in breeding hybrids of cotton, pearl millet (bajra), castor and pigeon pea (arhar). After China, we have also made breakthrough in hybrid rice technology.

Biotechnology will be the science of the 21st century. Genetic engineering holds vast potential both for increasing productivity and conserving our natural resources. Support to both public and private sector initiatives in biotechnology is crucial at this juncture. India is fortunate to have created a separate Department of Biotechnology, which is laying greater emphasis on both research and human resource development to make our public system strong. Considering new options and opportunities that this new science offers, we need to move aggressively to reap the likely benefits. Also the application of biotechnology must address concerns for bio-safety and protect the interests of our resource poor farmers. The research agenda must clearly address both benefits and the concerns. Besides biotechnology, the challenge to double our food production in the next decade would require application of all other sciences for sustainable advances in crop, animal and aquatic productivity and for strengthening our food health and livelihood security system.

As both population and standard of living rise, the overall demand for energy will also rise dramatically. It is forecast to double by 2025. Besides tapping new sources, we may have to adopt energy conservation technologies vigorously. India has, over the years, successfully used nuclear energy and techniques for peaceful purposes. As the agricultural operations become more energy demanding, the role of nuclear power as a source of energy would become more important. Isotopic and radiation methods have been extensively used to measure and monitor nutrients and water in the soil-crop system. Similarly, radiation has been used to create genetic variability in desired characters to breed new varieties that have higher yield, improved resistance to diseases and tolerance to abiotic stresses. Now we shall have to use these techniques more for post-harvest management and value addition in future.

Power generation from renewable energy sources such as solar, wind, tide, biogas and biomass is becoming increasingly attractive, though their capacity to meet the overall energy demand is assessed to be marginal. The options of commercial development of fusion power, accelerator driven reactors, agri-electronics, bio-diesel, alcohol for running tractors and engines, gasification of biomass for thermal and mechanical application, fuel technology for electricity generation and stand alone power units to run on biomass etc. need to be vigorously perused. But all these options will require effective partnership, both national and international.

Similarly, the role of space technology and other tools of research such as Geographic Information System (GIS) and crop modelling in ensuring productivity estimates for food security is also need to use remote sensing to discriminate crops suffering from various stresses with those of diseases. If space technology can be directed to forecast natural calamities such as droughts, floods, cyclone etc., or assess their adverse impact, we can obviously take up effective contingency measures, including insurance against crop failures.

Even there is a big gap between the yields obtained in the research fields and those in the farmers' fields, which need to be bridged through a revamped extension system that ensures minimum technology dissemination loss. Hence, a dedicated cadre of technology agents will be required to effectively transfer the modern technologies that are blended with traditional knowledge and wisdom. The use of modern information and Communication Technology (ICT) for the dissemination of new and sustainable eco-friendly technologies through innovative institutional mechanisms like Agri-clinics will accelerate the transfer of technology (TOT) process in future.

The vast potential available with non-crop and non-food grain enterprises to enhance income, provide employment and improve nutrition remains under exploited. Changing consumption and demand patterns and new trade opportunities have provided impetus to greater diversification and farming system allowing more emphasis on horticulture, milk, poultry, fish and other animal products, fibres, mushroom, spices and condiments, medicinal and aromatic plants and agro-forestry. In this context, value addition, post production technology and agri-business aspects would require greater scientific input including optimal use of social management sciences.

Focus on improving efficiency also implies stress on post-production management, value addition, minimization of losses, processing, storage, observing sanitary and phytosanitary measures, packaging, transport and marketing, agro-industry and agri-business. Efficient utilization of vast quantity of crop residues and byproducts will be highly beneficial provided we generate appropriate technologies that suit our conditions.

Permanency

Permanency is a reflection of sustainable agricultural development while ensuring conservation of our natural resources. Hence, technologies that are around sustainable farming systems with least dependence on costly inputs, including chemicals, will have to be promoted in future. Improving input use efficiency would also be a key factor for attaining permanency. A paradigm shift in our research agenda focusing more on systems' approach rather than commodity-oriented research will be critical for sustaining agriculture in future.

In future, a twin pillar strategy centred around : first, genetic enhancement involving genes that can ensure responsiveness to low inputs and also biotic and abiotic stresses, and second, efficient production management through agronomy and agri-engineering practice would be central to sustainable agriculture. Emphasis will have to be laid more now on precision farming, conservation tillage, use of stress tolerant genotypes, input (soil, water, fertilizer, seeds, pesticides, energy etc.) use efficiency and blending of our rich traditional knowledge with that of modern science etc.

We are also rich in our bio-diversity and possess valuable genes for both biotic and abiotic stresses. However, we are losing our bio-diversity at historic rates with potentially catastrophic but as yet uncertain consequences. We also have to protect our rich plant, animal and fish genetic resources through appropriate conservation technologies and IPR regime. The recent success in protecting our rights for *neem, haldi* and *basmati* rice provide us the much needed confidence to guard against such threats in future. We need to have appropriate IPR regime and *sui generis* systems which can provide legal instruments to protect available genetic resources.

Overexploitation of natural resources to increase agricultural production is also required to be checked through research on management of climate, soil, water, plants and animals. The *el nino*, super cyclone, and global climate change are emerging as serious threats that would need disaster managements strategy based on scientific intervention. Also the problem of contaminants, effluents and waste management needs to be addressed through eco-friendly technologies.

We must conserve both our soil and water resources through appropriate land use planning and monsoon management strategy. To obviate the problems of soil health, and integrated plant nutrient management (IPNM) approach assumes significance, which would require an integrated, inter-disciplinary and inter-departmental effort. Balanced use of chemical nutrients with organic fertilizers on soil test based recommendations can ensure long range productivity and economic returns. We also need to place greater emphasis on residue management, legumes as intercrops, and bio-fertilizers. Our focus must now be more on management rather than on manufacture of fertilizers. Similarly, to combat diseases and pests we will have to adopt aggressively the integrated pest management (IPM) technologies. In this endeavour, synergistic use of resistance crop varieties, appropriate cultural practices, application of biopesticides and use of biocontrol agents will be necessary.

Integrated watershed management is now an accepted rational approach for sustainability for our ecosystems through restoration of degraded soils, efficient water harvesting and improvement in an overall productivity. In this context, the first and foremost need is to have an integrated approach involving the people and the R&D institutions to provide required technical backstopping.

Policies

Appropriate policies are evidently the most powerful instruments to accelerate economic development. Thanks to the unstinted support and encouragement given by successive Prime Ministers from Pandit Jawaharlal Nehru to Shri Atal Bihari Vajpayee, both agricultural research and concern for poverty received priority attention. Recent announcement of the National Agricultural Policy is yet another testimony to this. It has targeted 4 per cent annual growth in agricultural sector which is a precursor to alleviating poverty, increasing employment and overall national economic development.

The situation of surpluses and low commodity prices in recent years have somehow lulled us into a false sense of security — a belief that the agricultural revolution has been won and will continue to be with us. Such complacency could be catastrophic, especially in view of the fact that we will have to feed 300 million additional people by 2020, requiring additional 100 million tonnes of foodgrains. Also the investment by national governments and international agencies in agricultural research and development is reflecting a declining trend. At the same time, it is unreasonable to expect that the private sector will either invest heavily or focus mainly on the problems of the rural poor. We, therefore, see a vital role for our national government and the international agencies to continue investing in agricultural research. Therefore, investment in scientific research means harvesting both peace and prosperity.

Rural oriented policies are needed to create conditions for adopting improved technologies. Since most of our land holdings are small and fragmented, the programmes of land reforms and development should be given high priority. Consolidation of holdings, freeing the lease market for land, updating and improvement of land records, computerization and issue of land pass books to the farmers will, obviously, give a fillip to farm investments.

We also need to accelerate the flow of institutional agricultural credit and public investment in developing rural infrastructure such as minor irrigation (especially shallow wells), roads, electrification, markets, etc. On rural credit, self held groups need to be promoted along with micro-financing.

The new world trade regime, following formation of WTO, has also thrown many challenges. As GATT negotiations were being finalized, we had hoped that liberalized of trade would provide large scope for promoting farm income as well as growth of Indian agriculture. The last few years have dispelled all such expectations. There has been a sharp decline in international agricultural prices since 1976. The dollar value of farm export earnings has also declined since then and domestic prices rule higher than the international prices, which has make imports attractive. The country has been placed in a piquant situation — with a feeling of uncertainty and despondence among Indian farmers who feel threatened by the unstable economic environment following liberalization. Obviously, the new trade regime would require trade regulation initiatives on tariffs, quick response to dumping and aggressive negotiations in the forthcoming trade talks on subsidies in developed agriculture, neo-protection through sanitary and phyto-sanitary (SPS) restrictions and social clauses. On domestic front, we need to improve efficiency of domestic production and more importantly of marketing and processing. Beside improvements in technology, this would require domestic policy reforms and strong emphasis on improvement in infrastructure. Quality improvements, SPS, quarantine, market intelligence, IPR and international technology access, etc. would substantially upgrade our capability to meet the new challenges.

Producing enough food is not the sufficient condition for social welfare. Food must reach to the poorest of the poor. In the past, several government-sponsored programmes were launched to meet the food availability and nutritional security in rural areas. These programmes were effective in alleviating poverty and improving our food security. In the new economic regime, these programmes be viewed in the context of livelihood security. Poor must be protected to meet his basic needs.

Partnership

Mutual interdependence and strong complementarities at various levels of scientific pursuit, information dissemination and development process make it imperative to solicit partnership from the grassroots to the international level. This partnership refers to : (i) involvement of local people in problem identification, research planning, technology generation and technology transfer, (ii) involving NGOs and other voluntary organizations and local institutions, (iii) linkages among private sector, industry and public sector research systems and institutions, and (iv) knowledge sharing and technical cooperation at the international level.

There is an obvious need to reorient our research in a consultative mode by involving all the stakeholders. Research planning should shift from 'top down' to 'bottom up' approach. This paradigm shift is extremely important to focus on need based research that is consistent with the farmer's operating environment, constraints, and resource availability. Similarly, NGOs and other organizations can also be of great help in identifying need based research agenda and effective transfer of technology.

The entire scientific environment is becoming highly challenging and complex requiring strong inter-disciplinarity and more dependence of basic and fundamental sciences. We have to shed compartmentalization approach and forge interaction among various scientific organizations like ICAR, CSIR, DRDO, ISRO, ICMR, BARC, ICSSR and universities etc.

There are certain areas such as biotechnology where scientific advances can be much faster through private sector involvement. Private sector and industry have also the comparative advantage in multiplying, provisioning and marketing the end products ensuring required benefits to the ends users. We need to create viable, legal, remunerative and enabling environment for participation of the private sector in order to realize our goal of food, nutrition and environmental security.

Given the commonality of problems faced by most of the countries in agricultural production and development, it is useful to cross fertilize various experiences. Moreover, ensuring food and nutritional security, efforts towards healthy environment are being made by a number of countries. Thus, sharing of knowledge, resources and facilities and scientific exchanges would be mutually rewarding. In such efforts, arrangements like providing of networks, establishment of virtual laboratories, knowledge platforms and linkages — national and international would play a significant role towards food, nutrition and environmental security. Global partnership is also needed to address the problems transcending national boundaries like global warming, cyclones, earthquakes etc. Science aiming at the international public good research obviously requires global partnership on principles of mutual trust and benefit sharing.

Epilogue

We all know that any national development comes from years of dedicated efforts and ingenuity — step by step, experiment by experiment, course correction by course correction and application by application.

The science had always been the vanguard of past successes. In order to transform not only the agriculture but the entire national economy, we shall need new science. New science would demand new innovative approaches and the new problems shall demand new solutions. Therefore, we must act fast to bring in decisive change that can ensure as quick wins.

All these would be possible, if right institutions are in place, right human resource is available, enabling environment exists, inter-institutional, inter-regional and inter-national linkages exist and access to knowledge, both new and traditional is blended together. It is the technology led society with competent human resources that we need to build and nurture, or else we shall lag behind. There has to be a paradigm shift from input based technology to resource conservation technology. Our demonstrated strengths in science through Green and White revolution, atomic power, satellite launch, missile test, ICT revolution etc., are some of the visible indicators of science led progress. These advancements give us the confidence about our scientific might and reflect that Indian Science in the new millennium will lead and not just follow. For required technological innovations, public scientific organizations are fully geared to demonstrate our ability to convert the challenges into opportunities. With these strengths, we have excelled in the past and being an optimist, come what may, we shall face the new challenges successfully in future as well and make India hunger free and environmentally safe.

2

Biodiversity Conservation and Sustainable Agriculture

Introduction

THE ENORMOUS variety of life-forms and their associations is called biological diversity, or in short, biodiversity. The term is defined by the Convention on Biological Diversity as *the variability among living organisms from all sources, including terrestrial, marine and others aquatic ecosystems, and the ecological complexes of which they are part; this includes diversity within species, between species, and of ecosystems*. More simply, biodiversity is the variety of the life-forms including their genetic make-up and all kinds of their assemblages.

The complexity and diversity of life are manifested in the variety of forms and functions of organisms, and their communities. At one level, the organisms and their populations are distinct from one another in terms of their unique genetic make-up, handed down by evolution across generations. At another level, biodiversity expresses itself in the variety of associations of the organisms interacting among themselves and with the environment for utilising resources.

Components of Biodiversity

Species diversity

Species are groups of natural populations of organisms that are reproductivity isolated from other such groups. Although this definition is difficult to apply to asexually reproducing organisms and extinct (fossil) organisms, the absence of evidence of interbreeding is still held to be the main criterion of identifying species.

The status of biodiversity is generally measured in terms of the species richness in a given habitat or location. Species richness describes the total number of species — whether wild or domesticated — occurring within a geographical area. Tropical ecosystems are more species-rich than temperate area.

Recent estimates indicate that between 10 million and 30 million species, are likely to be existing currently on earth, of which 73 per cent are bacteria, and 18 per cent are flowering plants. Insects account for about 76 per cent of all animals, of which about 60 per cent are beetles. Tens of millions of species are remaining to be described.

Taxic diversity

Species diversity estimates do not provide the complete picture of the diversity of kinds of organisms : it only gives the total number of species. The relative abundance of species in various taxonomic groups (trees, birds, mammals, beetles) is understood by taxic diversity. For example, an island with two species of birds and a species of frog is more diverse than another island with three species of birds and no frog, although the species diversity in both the islands are equal.

Genetic diversity

Individuals of sexually reproducing species are different in their genetic endowment from each other. Random mutations or changes in genes stored in sex cells are the primary sources of genetic variability, and the rate of mutations appear to be constant for individual genes. As a result of genetic recombination and mutations accumulated over millions of years, each species contains a stupendous amount of genetic information (*species gene pool*). Genetic diversity of individuals within a population and that among populations within a species comprise the genetic diversity of a species.

Genetic diversity allows a species to adapt over time to the environmental changes — through evolving disease resistance, tolerance to climatic stresses, mechanisms for predator avoidance, etc. The loss of populations or subpopulations through habitat destruction or environmental poisoning and other current anthropogenic factors cause genetic erosion, narrowing the evolutionary options of the species.

In contrast, human communities in the past have nurtured and increased the genetic diversity of the species which they had domesticated. Hybridisation and selection experiments conducted by humans have expanded the genetic diversity of a number of crops and domesticated animals. Thus, populations of the Indian rice *Oryza sativa var. indica Linn*. have been experimentally inter-crossed for obtaining different combinations of traits by generations of unnamed farmer-breeders, to produce over 42,000 landraces, most of which have been replaced in modern agriculture by high-yield varieties (HYV). Genetic diversity in the wild relatives of domesticated crops and animals must be conserved as a crucial element of biodiversity, because they can be used to improve on different desirable traits of modern crop cultivators and animal breeds that have reduced genetic variability.

Ecosystem diversity

The existence of a number of species and the biological interactions among them determine the structure of an ecosystem. Thus an enormous diversity of ecosystems forms a part of biodiversity.

Conventionally, ecosystems are broadly described in three categories — terrestial, freshwater, and marine. Most of the standard biodiversity estimates have been made on different types of terrestrial ecosystems. It is generally supposed that 80 per cent of all species are terrestrial, and that tropical rainforests hold a major proportion of species diversity. However, recent deep sea explorations indicate that the biological diversity of the sea floor communities might rival that of the tropical rainforest biome.

Therefore, conservation of the ecosystem is essential for conserving a species. Habitat destruction and fragmentation, chemical pollution, and overexploitation of component species are the most immediate anthropogenic threats to ecosystems.

Threats of Biodiversity

The extinction of a species is generally due to multiple causative factors, and no single threat to species populations can be considered independently. Threats may be anthropogenic or natural.

Natural extinction threats

The past episodes of extinction of species, and even of entire taxonomic classes of species, are known to have taken place due to meteorological and geological catastrophes — the causes remaining controversial — volcanic eruptions, meteor impacts, and accumulated global climate change. The largest of the mass extinctions occurred at the end of the Permian era, ca. 250 million years ago (MYA), which eliminated 80 per cent of the entire marine animal genera.

Apart from these episodes of mass extinctions there is a presumed "background" rate of natural extinction of species. Background extinction rates for organisms with narrow geographical ranges may have been higher than the average estimate, while that for widespread species is extremely low.

Threats from human activities

Current rates of extinctions are strikingly higher than the presumed average "background" extinction rates. Almost all of these extinctions have been due to the human impact. Unambiguous evidence of the anthropogenic extinction is furnished by comparisons of flora and fauna before and after the human appearance on Earth. Twenty mammals have already been recorded to have become extinct from the Earth in this century, and more than 2000 extinctions have occurred in the last 2000 years. At least 5366 animals and 26106 plants are globally threatened. However, these figures are highly conservative, since many millions of species are yet undescribed, and no assessment of their status is available. Apart from the species in the wild, numerous breeds of livestock and landraces of agricultural crops and threatened due to recent changes in land use patterns and replacement of indigenous varieties of crops and breeds of animals by exotic ones.

The anthropogenic causes of extinctions involve habitat destruction, habitat fragmentation, change in habitat quality, introduction of exotic species, and hunting and exploitation of species by humans. Anthropogenic loss of natural habitats seems to be the key ultimate cause of the present high rate of extinctions.

Habitat fragmentation may divide a previously more continuous population into small local subpopulations, long-term persistence of which becomes less likely. In recently and rapidly fragmented landscapes, migration between local populations is disrupted, enhancing the problems of inbreeding depression. The natural forging and breeding habits of a species may also become disrupted, resulting in a decline in population growth rate. Both habitat fragmentation and change in habitat quality entail extinction of a large range of small specialist who live in numerous microhabitats found only in large intact stretches of habitat.

Introduction of non-native organisms to new environments is second only to habitat destruction in causing destruction of native ecological communities. The spread of non-native organisms by humans has caused the spread of epidemics and extinctions.

In India, introduction of carps for intensive pisciculture has caused extinction of native fishes like *Schizothorax spp*. The practice of intoxication of pisciculture ponds for weeding out non-culturable fish has also caused local extinction of an unestimated number of fish, frogs and invertebrates. Similarly, thousands of landraces of indigenous rice are known to have disappeared from the country due to the modern practice of monocultures of a few exotic hybrid rice varieties.

Overkill and overexploitation of organisms by humans constitute a special cause of extinction of species. For instance, extinction of the cheetah in India has been due to the combined effect of habitat destruction and hunting.

Why Conserve Biodiversity?

The value of biodiversity may be roughly estimated by considering the economic, ecological, anthropological, recreational and epistemic benefits derived from it.

Economic benefits

All the items of our food, excepting water and mineral salts, comes from natural biodiversity. For example, until the invention of plastic polyfibres (nylon, decron, polyester), all the fibres for garments have been biotic in origin — wool, cotton, fax, jute, mestha, varieties of hemp and silk. Another example would be the fact that all the drugs and medicines so far discovered, excepting a few mineral and synthetic ones, are of biotic origin.

Ecological services

Various organisms play numerous crucial roles in ecosystem function, and all the functions of a species are not fully comprehended in the current state of our knowledge. However, there is an increasing body of evidence to indicate that removal of at least certain "keystone species" would severally affect the ecosystem functions. The elimination of such species can bring about a cascade of destruction.

Cultural-anthropological utility

Apart from the direct uses of biodiversity for subsistence and market economy, local communities have elaborate requirements of various elements of biodiversity for religious and cultural purposes.

Many indigenous cultures have a built-in "eco-logic". Cultures of hunter-gatherers and shifting cultivators almost invariably pose themselves as natural components of the ecosystem they live in. These cultures seem to recognise the bequest value of the natural heritage, and uphold a community responsibility for conserving their ancestral ecosystems for future generations. Erosion of biodiversity would inevitably result in the loss of local knowledge systems, and destruction of cultural diversity. Conversely, the erosion of cultural diversity would lead to the disappearance of the many life-forms and ecosystem which have been preserved by these cultures through traditional mechanisms of conservations.

Recreational and aesthetic utility

Many scientists have argued that humans have an inherent psychological need for, and aesthetic inclination toward, natural environment, and that the aesthetic preference of certain landscapes and species is a result of natural selections. Wilderness areas, including sanctuaries, national parks and biosphere reserves therefore have an immense recreational value, in addition to their other functions.

Agricultural Biodiversity

Fifteen thousand years ago our ancestors were using thousands of kinds of plants for nourishment. The transition to agriculture necessarily caused that number go decrease. As people began to domesticate crops the number of plant sources they depended on decreased. But at the same time the diversity within each crop increased as the domesticated crops came to fit into the myriad environments to which they were exposed. In other words, early farmers reduced the number of species used for food, but traditional farming practices steadily increased the diversity within those species through accidental and intentional cross-breeding and selection. In India for example, the mango, *Mangifera indica*, has been bred to create 1000 varieties, and some 100,000 varieties exist of one species of rice. However, it is the interdependence of each variety with its ecological and socio-cultural setting which defines its ability to contribute to the overall goal of sustainable food production. In history this has been managed with optimum efficiency.

However today with a rapidly growing human population and changing consumption patterns, the evolution of agriculture from traditional to modern, intensive systems, has been stimulated. The late 1960s witnessed the emergence of agricultural systems that emphasised maximising crop yields and uniformity and standardisation of farming systems, varieties and technologies. This approach, which entailed a greater use of energy, agricultural chemicals and mechanisation, was subsequently dubbed the *Green Revolution.*

Nonetheless, while modern agriculture has brought huge gains in food production, it is also responsible for considerable damage to biological diversity. The consequence of the introduction of new varieties of crops through genetic engineering, cross-breeding etc., has been the replacement and loss of traditional, highly variable, farmers' varieties. Diversity has been affected through three main types of impacts :

(a) On the genetic variability of the managed plant or animal species which can be manipulated with modern genetic engineering methods.

(b) On the natural ecosystem where agriculture takes place (or which it has displaced). (For example, one effect is the reduction of organic matter through tillage for crops; another is the reduction of biotic and structural complexity at the landscape level. Agriculture is the largest single cause of habitat conversion.)

(c) Through off-site pollution or alternation, such as by siltation, chemicals or invasive species.

Agricultural Diversity in India, China and USA

India	India once had 30,000 varieties of rice; today 75 per cent of the rice production comes from 10 varieties.
China	In 1949, China had 10,000 varieties in use; by the 1970s, only 1000 were in use.
United States	Approximately 97 per cent of food plant varieties available to United States Farmers no longer exist.

Conservation of Agricultural Biodiversity : Why?

Modern commercial agriculture focused its attention on developing a smaller number of crop varieties which were then widely disseminated. This approach has been widely successful as biotechnology has soared to amazing heights. One other effect of the replacement of traditional agricultural crop varieties, has also been the economic growth of the seed industry. Ever since the Green Revolution, agriculture has become more about economic success and extreme crop production, rather than its professed purpose of being able to feed everyone in the world.

Many multinational profit-hungry seed companies like Monsanto and Cargill have consequently come into existence. Recently these seed companies have collaborated to lobby for seed-patenting laws — laws allowing a company to obtain a "patent" on a new variety of lettuce or tomato, for instance. To be enforceable, these laws require that the new, patented variety be internally consistent and uniform. This quest for increasing uniformity is yet another factor contributing to the narrowing of the genetic base for crops. *Uniformity, as a pattern of production, becomes inevitable only in the context of control and profitability.*

On course, distribution of the new seeds would not have necessarily caused extinction of traditional varieties were those varieties collected for *ex situ* conservation as they were replaced. But the crop breeding institutes have only been collecting the old varieties seriously since 1970. And seed companies have not yet acknowledged that their responsibility may include seeing that the seeds they displace do not become extinct.

Today, for example, it is estimated that high-yield varieties (HYVs) are now used in 52 per cent wheat growing areas. In the Punjab and West Bengal, the area under HYV wheat is 100 per cent. Recently, the United Nation's Food and Agricultural Organisation (FAO), warned of a drastic decline in the diversity of crop plants all over the world. India, for example, once had 30,000 varieties of rice, but today, 75 per cent of rice production comes from only 10 HYVs.

Is this loss of diversity necessarily a bad thing? Increasing genetic uniformity in agriculture is the main problem even though by modern agricultural methods, this genetic uniformity is advantageous in securing greater yields and for specifically desired morpho-agronomic cultivators.

For example, typically, today's plant breeder will search for one major gene to confer resistance on a few variety. However, breeding in this kind of complex resistance is too time-consuming, complicated, and costly to the modern breeder.

By utilising one-gene resistance (even if made necessary by the pressure to get something on the market quickly), the plant breeder gives pests or diseases an easy target, with only one line of defense to get around. This danger of uniformity has been instanced quite a few times in history, for example, the Irish potato famine of the 1940s and the Pearl millet wipeout which led to starvation in India by downy mildew in 1971, and the recent crisis in the rice fields of South Àsia due to the widespread Rice Stunt infection.

The virtue of possessing traditional varieties may also be seen in the example of Zambia where 90 per cent of the domestic needs of maize were grown through the use of highly uniform hybrid maize cover. In 1974, however, a new mould attacked the crop and 20 per cent of the hybrids were infested, while the impact on traditional maize was negligible. This is a concrete example of the strength of natural diversity. Recent studies in West Bengal show that a dramatic increase in rice pests and diseases after the introduction of HYVs.

Thus, for many farming communities, diversity, be it social, cultural, or genetic, means security. Genetic diversity provides security for the farmer against pests, disease and unexpected climatic conditions. It also helps small scale farmer to maximise production in the highly variable environments in which they traditionally used to cultivate their crops. Higher yields are obtained from employing a mixture of crops and crop varieties, each one specifically adapted to the micro-environment in which it grows, rather than by using one of few 'modern' varieties. Such uniform varieties will only reach their potential if the environment is also uniform. That means high quality land, where the fertility and water status have been evened out with the use of fertilizers and irrigation, all generally unavaible to the small scale farmer. However, the use of inorganic fertilisers has led to the growing crisis of soil erosion and depletion of soil quality. Likewise, use of year-round irrigation by large numbers of pumps has led to severe depression of the water table. Major irrigation projects brought by big dams on rivers have caused more ecological and social problems than solving them.

Uniform cropping pattern is often less productive in marginal areas. Besides, genetic diversity provides farming communities with a range of products with multiple uses. Some varieties of a particular crop may be good for immediate consumption, others for long term storage, yet others for pest resistance, and so on. This genetic wealth is, in addition, an important reservoir of diversity for agriculture worldwide, providing important characteristics for pest and disease resistance, nutritional quality and other factors.

Based on thousand of years of experience and a deep knowledge of their needs and their agricultural production systems, communities have developed multiple strategies for their farming systems, like intercropping and agroforestry. Traditional farming systems use several varieties of each crop.

For cereals like sorghum, rice, wheat and barley, which are self-pollinated, and for vegetatively propagating crops like potatoes and bananas, the number of varieties used may be very high.

As globally there is a growing ecological awareness among consumers, and since there is a greater demand for chemical-free food, local farmers' varieties, which have evolved free of chemicals are the best choice for organic farming and other alternative agricultural practices.

Threats to Sustainable Agriculture

Biotechnology (genetic engineering)

The principles of biotechnology may be traced to 10,000 years back, in the form of selective breeding experiments. In fact, researchers using the latest biotechnology methods, which enable the transfer of a gene from one organism to another, are basically working with the same scientific processes. People have used several methods, which progressed according to the scientific developments over centuries to increase crop productivity, improve the food supply and produce better foods. But genetic engineering (the ability to transfer genetic information between species) is different from breeding methods in the sense that in the former one can cross species to form hybrids at the genetic level. For a country like India, genetic engineering can increase food production, especially when the number of mouths to feed is ever increasing. However, though HYVs and hybrid strains may increase productivity, the issue of conserving diversity must be considered for long term sustainability. Biotechnology should be geared towards working with the inherent diversity existing on the plant, rather than attempting to globalise single varieties which may be completely unadapted to environments alien to its local settings.

Chemicalisation

Chemical fertilisers are an important input of agriculture, as they provide additional nitrogen, potassium and phosphorus to crops. Their use in optimal quantities is essential to maintain the fertility of the land and to obtain the benefit of HYV seeds. Due to limited availability of land, fertilisers are all the more important for increased yield and increased profits to farmers. A vast array of pesticides, insecticide and herbicides working against insects and disease also are now available. They also have an important role in food production and disease control. However, chemical control has achieved a bad reputation as a biologically detrimental option. Insecticides are seen as extremely damaging to the environment. They are known to leave toxic residues in the soil, are not usually selective in their effects, (when they kill both beneficial and harmful insects) in contributing to eutrophication, are toxic to human, and so on. Herbicides and fungicides are generally less environmentally damaging, but still inflict subtle, deleterious effects.

Nonetheless, until alternative forms of pest control or fertiliser use, like biological control, or biofertilisers, are fully researched and become economically viable options, chemicals are likely to spread. Therefore, we need to rapidly evolve alternatives without chemical.

So the pursuit of more sustainable forms of agriculture is a central importance in meeting the challenge of biotechnology. Do we grow our crops with genetically engineered resistance to polluting herbicides or do we develop ecological forms of agriculture which work with the rhythms and cycles of nature to achieve the same end of feeding humanity?

Proven alternatives to commercial agriculture exist in many parts of the world. Documentation during the past decade has shown that these alternative agricultural technologies are productive, economical, resource-conserving, and appropriate to many farming situations in both industrialised and developing countries. These alternatives are known by many names including organic farming, eco-agriculture, biological farming, bio-dynamic agriculture, indigenous farming systems, and agro-foresty systems. Nonetheless, although there are more than 30,000 alternative farms in the US, these make up less than 1 per cent of the total population of farms.

Another term study by Washington University researchers has shown that alternative agriculturists, using only 40 per cent energy, made as much net income as conventional farmers. These alternative farmers also suffered less erosion damage than the conventional farmers. Water pollution is also consequently minimised.

Of course, alternative agriculture must have the support of consumers who will purchase the produce. This fortunately seems to be the trend today. In the US alone, 11.4 million households are interested in organic gardening methods, 36 million of which use "organic nutrient sources" in their gardens in addition to commercial fertilisers. The millions of adherents to environmentalism and the appropriate technology are natural allies of alternative agriculturists. Export of Indian tea grown in chemical-free gardens find much higher demand in the international market than conventional grown tea.

3

Diverse Women for Diversity

ECONOMIC GLOBALIZATION is sweeping across the world, making the gap between the rich and the poor wider and deeper, increasing the spread of cultural and biological monocultures, and increasing the vulnerability of both ecosystems and social systems to breakdown and disintegration. New epidemics are emerging, old ones are resurging, creating a major crisis in public health. Economic crises have caught entire economies by storm, leading to massive unemployment. More and more societies are trapped in religious, ethnic and cultural warfare. The end of this century is clearly a period of severe violence and dislocation.

Women's energies are needed to shape the new millennium on the basis of peace in place of violence, justice in place of deepening inequality, sustainability in place of non-sustainable exploitation of the earth's resources and a cultural and biological diversity in place of monocultures and homogenisation.

Third World women have a special role to play at this historical moment, since they pay the highest price and are the worst victims. Women of the South pay the highest price for economic Globalization in terms of food insecurity and health insecurity. They loose the most knowledge, or skills and livelihoods when technologies are introduced, when their knowledge is appropriated through 'biopiracy' and intellectual property rights. They are the worst victims of civil wars, ethnic and religious violence. And they pay the biggest price through increasing poverty under Globalization and structural adjustment programmes.

While the women of the South bear the worst burden in terms of the costs of Globalization, they also have the experience to build alternatives. Since Globalization is also the Globalization of poverty, food insecurity and social disintegration, women's experiences from the South can help build a global response to economic Globalization in all its dimensions.

In recent years the global expression of women's concerns has had a Northern bias. In Cairo and a Beijing the differences between the North and the South were apparent. Instead of letting our concerns be marginalised, we would like to build an international coalition of women acting in coherence on issues that concerns the women of the South most-food security, health security, economic security, environmental security and peace. These are also the issues that most affect the future of people and the planet, and the issues from which women have been excluded in global decision-making.

We Would Like to :

1. Articulate our concerns on *our* terms, from *our realities,*
2. Intervene in the most urgent economic, political and environmental issues at the international level with collective strength,
3. Find our partners in the North on the basis of our priorities and processes initiated by us.

Third World women hold the highest potential for creating alternatives for peace, justice and sustainability. While being South-centred, the women centred plurality of alternatives will also be based on South-North solidarity and gender solidarity. Diverse Women for Diversity thus begins in the South, but is based on an inclusive philosophy of ever-widening circles of transformation and change.

The Value of Diversity

Violent technologies and a violent economic system are creating violent societies — with country after country sinking into a vicious cycle of economic insecurity and social decay and disintegration.

As ordinary women from across the world, we want this insanity and violence to end.

Making peace with diversity is fast becoming a survival imperative in our times of 'ethnic cleansing' and the spread of monocultures, in society and in nature.

Monocultures are an essential component of Globalization. Globalization is a recolonisation of life in all its diversity-cultural and biological.

This war against diversity is not entirely new. Diversity has been threatened whenever it has been seen as a threat and an obstacle. Violence and war are rooted in treating diversity as a threat, a disease, a perversion, a source of disorder. Globalization transforms diversity into a disease and deficiency because diverse systems cannot be brought under centralised control. Global control of raw materials and markets makes monocultures necessary.

Homogenisation and monocultures introduce violence at many levels. Monocultures are always associated with political violence, the use of coercion, control and centralisation. Without centralised control and coercive force, this world filled with the richness of diversity cannot be transformed into uniformity and homogenous structures, and without coercion and centralised control, these monocultures cannot be maintained. Self-organised and decentralised communities and ecosystems give rise to diversity. Globalization gives rise to coercively maintained monocultures.

Monocultures are also associated with ecological violence towards nature's diverse species. They are in fact a declaration of war against species. The violence does not cease with pushing species to extinction. It continues to be the mode of controlling and maintaining monocultures. Monocultures are vulnerable to ecological breakdown and are non-sustainable. Uniformity implies that a disturbance to one part of a system is translated into a disturbance to other parts. Instead of being contained, ecological de-stabilisation tends to be amplified. Sustainability and diversity are ecologically linked because diversity offers the self-regulation and multiplicity of interactions, which can heal ecological disturbance to any part of a system.

Women everywhere are active at the grassroots, creating and leading peace movements, ecology movements, and movements for socio-economic justice. Even while women and children are the worst victims of violence, inequality and environmental degradation, it is women who are taking the lead to provide alternatives based on peace, sustainability and justice. In spite of each of these movements having emerged separately, they are all connected to the possibility of diversity.

While reproductive rights have held attention since Cairo and Beijing, the economic and environmental rights for which women struggle in their everyday lives have been neglected both by international agencies and by the academy. There is urgent need to fill this vacuum at the international level. Women's thinking is providing alternative paradigms which are essential for providing alternatives in this period dominated either by the "TINA Syndrome" (there is no alternative) or by the approach that difference undermines any ground for solidarity and integration among people.

The movement of Diverse Women for Diversity is aimed at bringing the voices of women at the grassroots in diverse settings — to shape the millennium on the basis of the alternatives they have articulated and envisioned for peace and for environmental and economic rights. It is aimed at overcoming people's incapacity and hopelessness in the face of severe ecological, economic and political breakdown.

A global women's movement — which is a movement of movements, forming a coalition of grassroots responses on the most urgent issues of our time, needs to be strategically built on the basis of struggles and initiatives at the grassroots because the dominant paradigm of Globalization leaves purely local initiatives inadequate both in terms of providing alternative paradigms and alternative ways to act. The movement will build over two years to make the alternatives that women are creating and shaping as the foundation of human evolution in the next millennium based on peace, sustainability and justice. Thus, it will evolve in a participatory mode, building from the grassroots to the global, from the micro to the macro, and feeding back to the grassroots with new strength initiatives and information.

Linking the Grassroots with the Global

We aim at bringing together women from diverse regions and from different movements who are working on food security and health security, and conservation of biological and cultural diversity in the context of Globalization in a global coalition. We want to intervene collectively as women in some of the most significant issues of our time, with the women of the South and the women at the grassroots playing a leading role in agenda setting, prioritisation, actions and programmes. We want to continue our search for diverse solutions at the local level and a common defence at the global level. Some of us have been present on international negotiations while also being active in our local have been missing in the global processes related to peace making and peace keeping, economic Globalization and trade, biodiversity, biotechnology and intellectual property rights.

While women of the South are the primary custodians of biodiversity and the main actors related to biodiversity conservation, the women's organised collective voice has not been present in the processes related to the Convention on Biological Diversity (CBD), which was the treaty signed at Rio to protect biodiversity. We did, through the Women's Agenda 21, make a major difference to the Rio process, and would like to ensure that women's perspectives stay integral to the implementation of CBD.

Similarly, while most mobilisation on the impact of Globalization at the grassroots is led by women, women have not been a big presence at the World Trade Organisation (WTO), which is the trade body that was formed at the end of the Uruguay Round of GATT in 1995, where Globalization processes are decided and controlled.

We as women, have been active in evolving a South-centred, women-centred agenda for food security. Dr. Vandana Shiva with Prof. Maria Mies initiated the Leipzig appeal on Food

Security which became the basis of the Women's Day on Food at the NGO event at the World Food Summit. In 1991, as co-chair of the Women and Environment and Development Network, Dr. Vandana Shiva helped organise the Miami Congress on Women and Environment which led to the Women's Agenda 21, the major women's input in Agenda 21.

We now feel the need to build a global coalition of women who are engaged in grassroot networks but who are also influencing national and international policy in their respective fields. Besides linking the grassroots with the global, we also want to establish links between different networks which are more issue based, so that a coherent philosophy and strategy for change can evolve. It is this coherence in action and thought that will grow in a participatory process to shape a women's agenda for peace, justice and sustainability in the new millennium.

The Movement Programme

This proposal is aimed at building a global coalition of women as a collective process with particular focus on areas which most concern women in their everyday lives and in which networks already exist at the grassroots. Diverse Women for Diversity will connect the diversity networks across regions and across issues and sectors. Diverse Women for Diversity as a network of networks and a movement of movements will build, strengthen and integrate the networks in the following areas :

- (a) Women's Food Security Networks
- (b) Women's Biodiversity and Biotechology Networks
- (c) Women's Knowledge, Community Rights and Intellectual Property Rights' Networks
- (d) Women's Health Networks
- (e) Women's Globalization and Economic Diversity Networks
- (f) Women's Peace and Cultural Diversity Networks

In each of these areas, women are primary actors at the grassroot level but are missing as a force when it comes to global decision-making processes. In addition, women in different regions and different issues are not able to come together as a collective force in global change. The project will contribute to this much needed coalition building.

The Diverse Women for Diversity movement have so far been built on locally available resources. However, organising women's energies and amplifying women's voices and visions to reach global decision-making during this critical point of transition to a new millennium (during a period of rapid transformation) requires an organised response.

Diverse Women will build global coalitions of locally embedded networks by facilitating the integration and coming together with ideas and actions that women are in any case generating at the grassroots. The Diverse Women movement will catalyse the global response by bringing together existing movements and networks active in the areas of food security, health, biodiversity, biotechnology, intellectual property rights, peach and alternative economic arrangements. The global coalition and collective articulation will then provide new strength and vigour to the movements at the grassroots. The leading network representatives will facilitate the work in each programme area and act as convenors for all activities and meetings.

(A) Women's Food Security Networks

The programme will build in the work on food security started at the Leipzig Conference and the World Food Summit and local initiatives to strengthen household, local and national food security. The ruling patriarchal paradigm states that free trade will generate food security. But women's experience shows that the market leaves out those who need food the most — children, women and the poor. The work programme on food security will, on the one hand, strengthen existing movements of women in the area of food security, and on the other hand, it will lead to an alternative to the free trade agenda of the WTO. The agreement on agriculture will be up for review in 2000. Women's organised input at the global level is necessary as a contribution to the review process.

Further, women's responses at the grassroots are also necessary to ensure household and community food security. The issue of food safety as an essential element of food security will connect the women's actions in the North and South, since food safety is becoming a major issue with "Mad Cow Disease" and the commercialisation of genetically engineered foods.

Outputs Expected :

- Participatory Documentation of Women's Food Security Alternatives,
- Monitoring of the Impact of Globalization and Agriculture and its impact on women and children,
- A Review of the Agriculture Agreement of the WTO from the perspective of Third World Women.

(B) Women's Biodiversity and Biotechnology Networks

On issues related to biodiversity and biotechnology, women have been the most influential in shaping alternatives to the global patriarchal paradigm based on irresponsible introduction of genetic engineering into the global good system and the appropriation of the world's biodiversity as the raw material for a handful of corporations.

An international legally biding protocol setting standards for the trade in genetically engineered organisms would be a crucial signal against deregulation of environmental and health security. There is an emerging conflict between CBD and security. There is an emerging conflict between CBD and GATT/WTO. An international legal framework on biosafety can stop the rat race towards deregulation serving comparative advantage at the detriment of the environment and human health. We as women want to engage in a conflict resolution between the Rio agendas for sustainability and equity and the WTO agenda for free trade and Globalization.

Outputs Expected :

- Participatory Documentation of Women's Resistance to Genetic Engineering,

- Women's Interventions in the Biosafety Negotiations and Meetings of WTO and Codex Alimentarious,
- A Network of Women Scientists to Monitor and Analyse the Impacts of Biotechnology on Health and the Environment.

(C) Women's Knowledge, Community Rights and Intellectual Property Rights' (IPRs) Networks

Five hundred years ago, women's knowledge was appropriated. Today, women's knowledge is once again being appropriated through 'biopiracy' — and women are being denied their status as 'knowers' and experts in knowledge related to biodiversity. Today it is women leading the movement against the new inquisition embodied in "Patents On Life". Women have led the referenda on "Patents On Life" in Switzerland and Austria. All women Members of European Parliaments (MEPs) — irrespective of parties, voted against the European Patent Directive.

The programme will be on women's knowledge built on women's perspectives on the sharing and monopolisation of knowledge and on patents on life and will create alternatives to the IPR system.

The programme will also provide a women's input for the Review of TRIPs in 1999.

Outputs Expected :

- A Women's Biopiracy Watch Network,
- Women's Perspectives on Knowledge, Community Rights and IPRs,
- A Review of TRIPs from the perspective of women, especially Third World Women.

(D) Women's Health Networks

The focus of the coalition building of Women's Health Networks will be :

1. Strengthening women's health traditions, especially their expertise in the knowledge and use of medicinal plants diversity,

2. Monitoring the impact of economic Globalization and structural adjustment on women's health,
3. Monitoring the 'biopiracy' of women's health knowledge,
4. Assessing the impact of IPRs on women's access to health care,
5. Discussion of the issue of cloning and reproductive rights.

Outputs Expected :

(a) Participatory Documentation of Women's Indigenous Health Traditions,

(b) Study of the Impact of Economic Globalization and Structural Adjustment on Women's Health,

(c) Analysis of the Impact of IPRs and Rights to health as an input to the Review of TRIPs in 1999.

(E) Women's Globalization and Economic Diversity Networks

Globalization, free trade, the liberalisation on imports and exports, are creating an economic monoculture. As the crisis of the South East Asian shows, economic monocultures are also vulnerable to major breakdowns triggered by small disturbances. Globalization is also creating a fictitious growth, with the virtual economy of US $3 trillion per day which is at least 6 times greater than the real economy of goods and services. The programme on Globalization and economic diversity will look at the impact of Globalization on women as well as the diverse economic options available through which women generate survival even while being excluded from the global market economy.

Outputs Expected :

(a) Reports on the Economic Impact of Globalization from the Grassroots,

(b) Women's Perspective on the Global Economy and on Economic Diversity and Economic Alternatives.

(F) Women's Peace and Cultural Diversity Networks

The programme on Peace and Cultural Diversity will focus on firstly, societies and contexts where the breakdown of peace is taking place under fundamentalism or terrorism, and secondly, on making women's interventions for peace stronger and more visible. The programme will also study the connections between economic Globalization, structural adjustment and violence in society.

***Diverse Women for Diversity* : Women's Food Security Network**

Leipzig Appeal for Women's Food Security

As a preparation to the World Food Summit, a FAO conference on Plant Genetic Resources took place in Leipzig, Germany in June 1996. At this conference, several women from the South and North observed that the whole discussion on Food Security did not take into account the fact that it is women worldwide who provide most food, both as producers and as consumers, to their families and their communities.

It was decided to formulate a statement rejecting the trend to remove food security from the hand of communities, farmers and to criticise the neoliberal policy of global food trade and the genetic manipulation of food for the sake of profit. They felt the need to present a critique from a women's perspective on the proposed policy of Globalization, liberalisation and industralisation of food production, trade and consumption. Therefore, an appeal was formulated and signed by Prof. Maria Mies and Dr. Vandana Shiva called "The Leipzig Appeal for Women's Food Security" which has first distributed in Leipzig Conference and later on circulated around the world. It received hundreds of signatures in support of this position.

Food Security in Women's Hands : Food Sovereignty for All, No to Novel Food and No to Patents of Life

For thousands of years, women have produced their own food and guaranteed food security for their children and communities. Even today, 80 per cent of the work in local food production in Africa is done by women. In Asia, 50-60 per cent and in Latin America, 30-40 per cent. And everywhere in the world, women are responsible for food security at the household level. In patriarchal society, however, this work has been devalued.

All societies have survived historically because they provide food security of their people. This policy, however, has been subverted by the Globalization, trade liberalisation, industrialisation and commercialisation of all agricultural products under the auspices of the World Trade Organisation (WTO) and the World Bank/IMF.

In November 1996, the UN's Food and Agriculture Organisation held a World Food Summit in Rome. Its goal is to achieve 'universal food security' by the year 2020, eradicating hunger and malnutrition. However, the technical preparatory papers show that this objective is to be met through a continuation and extension of industrialisation and the worldwide trade of food. Food will be produced where labour is cheapest and environmental protections weakest. Poor communities will be forced to produce luxury products for export to rich countries and classes. These trends are already in effect, with devastating results; large scale disappearance of small farmers, the end of food self-sufficiency, reliance on monoculture, genetic manipulation of food, loss of biodiversity and ecological sustainability. The impoverished rural people who are displaced through this world agriculture policy end up as marginal members of society in over-crowded, mega-cities without work, hope or food. Although it is known that this policy is the cause of poverty and malnutrition, it is still proposed as a remedy for these very ills. The most vulnerable groups affected by these policies are poor rural women and children.

This policy also threatens food and safety in the North, where the family farm has been rapidly replaced by chemical-intensive agribusiness. Consumers have become virtual hostages to a handful of food processing, and trading corporations. At the consumption end of the globalised food chain, women as housewives can no longer guarantee that they can give their families wholesome and healthy food.

In Peru, Chile and other countries of the South, women are fighting against this monopolistic policy, building their own communal food and health system. Women in indigenous societies fight against land alienation; women in export-oriented agriculture oppose hazardous chemicals. They are supported by women in the North who call for boycotts of these export products; flowers, vegetables, shrimps. Many groups in the North and South reject genetic manipulation of food. We are told that this biotechnology is necessary to feed a growing world population. However, 60 per cent of cereals are fed to animals in industrial farming systems. More and more land in the South is not used for nourishing local people, but for the production of luxury items for exports.

The commercial interests connected with this technology are particularly apparent in the promotion of patenting of life-forms — plants, animals and humans — under the protection of Trade-Related Intellectual Property Rights (TRIPs). In the South, the patenting of life-forms is opposed because it is in many cases based on simple piracy; theft of indigenous biodiversity and local knowledge. In the North, many people oppose patents on life-forms for ethical reasons.

On the consumer side, a majority of Europeans oppose genetically manipulated foods. Yet the European Union promotes such "novel food", even refusing to label it, thus denying consumers their human and civil right to determine what they eat. Consumption in this so-called "free market" becomes a matter of concern.

Worldwide, women are resisting the policies that destroy the basis of their livelihood and food sovereignty. They also create alternatives to guarantee food security for their communities based on different principles and methods than those governing the dominant, profit-oriented global economy. They are :

localisation and regionalisation instead of Globalization
non-violence instead of aggressive domination
equity and reciprocity instead of competition
respect for the integrity of nature and her species
understanding humans as part of nature instead of as masters of nature
protection of biodiversity in production and consumption

Food security for all is not possible within a global market system based on the dogma of free trade, permanent growth, comparative advantage, and competition and profit maximisation.

On the other hand, Food Security can be achieved if people within their local and regional economies feel responsible, both as producers and as consumers for the ecological conditions of food production, distribution and consumption, and for the preservation of cultural and biological diversity where self-sufficiency is the main economic goal.

Our food security is too vital an issue to be left in the hands of a few corporations with their profit motives, or up to national governments that increasingly loose control over food security decisions, or to a few — mostly male — national delegates at UN conferences who take decisions affecting all our lives.

Food Security must remain in Women's hands everywhere!

**And men must share the necessary work,
be it paid or unpaid.**

We have a right to know what we eat!

No to Novel Food and No to Patents on Life

**We will resist those who force us to produce and consume in ways
That destroy nature and ourselves!**

❑❑❑

4

Globalization of Food Insecurity

FOOD IS vital to survival. The production, distribution, preparation and even consumption of food has evolved over millennia from early hunting and gathering to the present ready-to-be-popped-into-the-microware foods available in giant superstores.

Each stage of the food system is replete with complexities, providing sustenance and survival options for millions of people. Policy changes affecting any one level of the food system after all the other levels, and thus have critical impact on the survival options of not just those who produce or work in the food system, but also of those who consume the food produced by the system.

The Current Global Food System

The end of the 20th century is characterised by the co-existence of two systems of food production, often represented by the West as modernity versus the past. One is capital intensive industrial agriculture that developed in this century in the West, the other comprises of many astonishingly intense systems of food production alongside systems which have evolved slowly over centuries, and which are still a feature of the less industrialized countries.

Industrial agriculture has led to mechanization replacing human and animal energy, monocultures replacing genetic diversity, large replacing small land holdings, and the development of new seeds through systematic plant breeding programmes — all in the name of science and 'efficiency'.

The combination of science and 'efficiency' is now leading to retailing and culinary industrialization and the beginning of the biological revolution of the land, *e.g.* through genetic engineering and modification, and in the factory *e.g.* enzyme use.

The 20th century food revolution has created new conflicts between the 'productionist' and 'consumerist' sectors : agri-business versus consumer-business; primary producers versus traders; production versus health.

Food Production and Globalization

Agriculture has been the longest lasting profession of humankind. Over millions of years, farmers of the world identified suitable crops, grew them, improved them through careful observation and selection, developed farming systems so suit their environment and their needs, produced surplus for batter and trade, all on the family farm.

With the industrialization of agriculture, size, capital intensive mechanization and agri-chemicals, as well as improved seed became equated with 'efficiency', particularly in the developed countries, sounding the death knell of the family farm and the family farmer.

Small farms continue to be the mainstay of agriculture in Third World countries. But they face the very real threat of extinction in the wake of globalization. Is the small farm worth preserving?

Public Value of Small Farms

The US Department of Agriculture, in its 1998 Report called *A Time to Act* prepared by its National Commission on Small Farms, noted the public value of small farms :

1. Diversity of ownership, of cropping systems, landscapes, biological organization, culture and traditions.
2. Environmental benefits. Responsible management of the natural resources of soil, water and wildlife.
3. Emprowerment and community responsibility. Decentralized land ownership, equitable economic

opportunity, greater social capital, increased sense of personal responsibility and feeling of control over one's life, increased accountability to community.

4. Places for families. Family farms can be nurturing places for children to grow up and acquire values, farming knowledge, skills and experience.
5. Personal connection to food through farmers' markets, community supported agriculture, and direct marketing.
6. Economic foundations. Small farms are vital to the economy.

The FAO acknowledged the value of the multiple functions of the small farms of Third World : "Concretely, by paying attention to the multiple function of agriculture and land use, all economic, social and environmental functions of agriculture, at multiple levels, are recognized and included in decision-making in order to promote synergy between these functions and to reconcile different stakeholder objectives".

One important reason for the continuance of the small farm is that it has always existed, in all cultures, in all environments, all over the world, developing crops and technologies to suit every environment and meet most needs.

The most important reason for keeping the small farm, however, is its productivity.

Productivity Issue

On the small farm, productive activities, labour mobilization, consumption patterns, ecological knowledge and common interests in long-term maintenance of the farm contribute to a stable and lasting economic and family-based enterprise, that makes for ecological stability, which is often socially reinforced by the community.

While the large farm today is being presented as the model of 'efficiency' due to 'economies' of scale of operation, there is increasing evidence from all over the world that the larger the farm, the more 'inefficient' it becomes, both in terms of resource utilization as well in terms of productivity.

Reasons for the Greater Productivity of Small Farms of the Third World

1. *Multiple Cropping*. Leading to more intensive use of space and time.
2. *Land Use Intensity*. Small farmers tend not to leave even a little land unused.
3. *Output Composition*. Larger farms are oriented towards land extensive enterprises like cattle grazing and extensive grain monoculture, while small farms emphasize labour and resource intensive use of land.
4. *Irrigation*. Small farmers tend to make more efficient use of irrigation.
5. *Labour Quality*. Small farmers are personally committed to the success of the farm while large farms use relatively alienated hired labour.
6. *Labour Intensity*. Small farms apply far more labour per unit area than do large farms.
7. *Input Use*. Small farms often use far more inputs per unit area than larger farms, particularly non-purchased inputs like manure and compost, unlike large farms where relatively more input like agrichemicals are purchased.
8. *Resource Use*. Small farms are more committed to management of other resources like forests and aquatic resources leading to increased and better quality of production.

Small Farm Productivity : Total Output *Vs.* Yield

'Yield' means the production per unit area of a single crop and thus hides the productivity of small farms, whose 'yields' are obviously low as they have less space to plant the single crop than large farms. It also hides the inefficiencies of the large farm — the bare ground between crops, where 'weeds' grow and have to be removed forcing the farmer to invest in or capital.

Small farms, in the Third World, fill the empty space with other crops, tend to combine or rotate crops and livestock, with manure serving to replenish soil fertility. Such integrated farming systems may produce less 'yield' of a one particular crop, but the total output per unit area (comprising the sum of everything the farmer produces — various crops and animal products) can be far higher.

Data shows that small farms almost always produce far more agricultural output per unit area than large farms everywhere in the world. Data specific to the United States shows that the smallest farms, those of 27 acres or less, have more than 10 times greater dollar output per acre than larger farms. While this in large part due to the fact that smaller farms tend to specialize in high-value crops, it also reflects relatively more labour inputs applied per unit area, and the use of more diverse farming systems.

Small Farm Efficiency

Small farms make more efficient use of land, while large farms, because of mechanization, have a higher labour productivity. If the 'total factor productivity' is taken into account, data from the 60s to the 80s show that small farms have greater total factor productivity farms in Sub-Saharan Africa, Asia, Mexico and Columbia and (later data) Honduras.

The case of the US is a little different. As very small farms cannot make full use of expensive equipment, they are generally inefficient; similarly, very large farms are also inefficient because of management and labour problems. Peak efficiency is likely achieved on mid-sized farms that have one or two hired labourers, but recent detailed analysis of true total factor productivity shows that larger farms are more inefficient than smaller farms, while very large farms are quite inefficient.

Small Farms in Economic Development

Farm production should generate, beyond grain, wealth for the overall improvement of rural life — better housing, education, health services, transportation, local business diversification, and more recreational and cultural opportunities.

Studies conducted from the 1940s onwards till as recent as 1996, show that large-scale corporate farming led to the death of nearby towns due to lack of employment opportunities and absentee ownership. Agricultural income was drained off into large cities to support distant enterprises, in contrast to places dominated by family farms, where the income circulated in nearby towns local business establishments, creating jobs and increasing and improving community prosperity, services and civic participation. This can be particularly seen in the Amish and Mennonite farm communities found in eastern United States.

Improving Social Welfare Through Land Reforms

Studies have also shown that redistribution of quality land to the landless and land poor rural families as part of development measures in Third World countries like Brazil, China, Taiwan have reduced poverty and improved human welfare. Data from the Landless Workers Movement in Brazil shows clearly that even if the government has to spend towards subsidizing these farmers, it is a lot less than what the government would spend if the population moved to towns and lived in urban slums. Other benefits include increased earning and drop in infant mortality among the beneficiaries.

National Economic Development and 'Bubble-up' Economics

Small farms have provided the basis for developing the economies of the industrialized countries, through the 'bubble up' process, which, unlike the 'trickle down' process offered by globalization for developing economies, has always worked. These small farms also helped to disperse political power, forming in themselves an important political base that politicians had to respond to.

Ecosystem Service : Resource Management, Biodiversity and Sustainability

Small farms, by their very nature, have to optimally utilize the environment for the survival. This means optimal use of land and water and preservation of biodiversity. In the United States, small farms devote 17 per cent of their area to woodland, compared to only 5 per cent on large farms, and maintain nearly twice as much of their soil improving uses including cover crops and green manure. In the Third World, small peasant farmers show a tremendous ability to prevent and even reserve land degradation, including soil erosion through developing farming systems and cropping partners to exploit site-specific characteristics without taking recourse to external and capital intensive inputs such as mechanization and agrochemicals. The main features of these systems are :

- farms are small in size with continuous production serving subsistence and market demands;
- maximum and effective use of local resources and low dependence on off-farm inputs;
- labour is skilled and complementary drawn largely from the household or community relations; it also shows a favourable energy input/output ratio;
- heavy emphasis on recycling of nutrients materials;
- building on natural ecological processes rather than struggling against them;
- diversified farm systems based on several cropping systems, featuring mixtures of crops, and crops with varietal and other genetic variability.
- minimizing risks to food security as well as improving nutritional content of food available through multicropping.

Traditional multiple cropping systems provide as much as 20 per cent of the world food supply.

As these agroecosystems are often located in centres of crop diversity, containing populations of variable and adapted landraces as well as wild and weedy relatives of crops, farmers cultivate numerous varieties of each crop, and thus become in-situ conservers of agricultural genetic diversity. In addition, these systems, through complex home gardens, and agroforestry, also become the genetic repository for other domesticated and undomesticated diversity — medicines, wood for multiple purposes, wild food, leaf litter, large and small liverstock, aquatic life, and wild life.

Inefficiencies of Corporate Agriculture

The produce by which corporate agribusiness had managed to create such conditions is basically through economic concentration where the aggregate of agriculture's new wealth has and continues to be consolidated in the hands of a few corporations and individuals.

This economic concentration that hides the economic inefficiencies of corporate agribusiness, takes four forms : market concentration, vertical concentration, conglomerate concentration and aggregate concentration, which themselves perpetuate myths of 'freedom' of the farmer, of the entrepreneur, and of enterprise itself.

Market Concentration

Market concentration in the food system exists when a few corporations control most of the markets existing in the system — the consumer market for foods, the farmer market for seeds and chemicals, the national markets that sell and buy food. They also control transport, milling, and processing. Three firms (IBP, Excel, Cargill's subsidiary, and ConAgro) control 81 per cent of the US beef packing industry and five firms control 75 per cent of the pork slaughter. In the commodity markets four firms control 59 per cent of port facilities, 62 per cent of flour milling, 74 per cent of wet corn milling and 76 per cent of soyabean crushing. Similarly, four firms again control 88.5 per cent of the $ 7 billion annual ready-to-eat cereal market.

Market concentration allows the conglomerates entrench myths of price competition, industrial growth, and of equitable income.

The Myth of Price Competition

There is no genuine price competition under market concentration. Actions like price cuts by one would negatively impact all. An unspoken monopoly agreement appears to exist among the corporations to maintain the price level, as exemplified by the case of ADM conspiring with competitors of domestic and world prices of lysine and citric acid to make even more money at the expense of customers, for, as an ADM employee put it, 'the competitor is our friend, the consumer is our enemy'.

The Myth of Industrial Growth

Market concentration leads, not to growth, but rather to a decline of the industry. Firstly, with no price competition, there is no incentive to reduce costs.

Secondly, the older a company grows, the more susceptible it becomes to the various forms of managerial diseconomies that range from rigid and wasteful hierarchical structures to resistance to change.

The Myth of Equitable Income

The acquisition of money has become an end in itself for corporations, rather than a means for people to equitably satisfy their needs, of which food is the most basic.

Thus, today, the income the farmer earns is far below the production costs, while the price the customer pays for the end product has no relevance to cost, efficiency, supply, demand, or fair market price — it is based on what agribusiness corporations can make him pay.

A key feature of market concentration is that fewer and fewer individuals make more and more of the economic decisions, which as a result is more anticompetitive, inefficient and harmful to the society as a whole.

Vertical Concentration

Vertical integration, which is market control in successive stages of production and distribution is clearly evident in agriculture and the food industry, where corporations have seedling-to-supermarket control over a variety of agricultural commodities.

Vertical concentration allows giant companies perform the dual role of supplying raw materials to non-integrated independents, and then competing with these independents in the sale of the final products, giving them the leverage to squeeze out competition, as well as control the food choices of the people.

Vertical integration lends itself to inefficiency in that the corporation often manufactures goods, better purchased from specialist suppliers, and thus accumulates extra management and overhead costs.

Conglomerate Concentration

This form of concentration can be defined simply as the possession of a large share of a given industry's resources or activity by companies that are primarily engaged in other industries but are not suppliers or users of the given industry's products. Two of the three largest food manufacturers in the US, the multinational tobacco companies Philip Morris and RJP Nabisco, are prime examples of this form of economic concentration. These companies manufacture both tobacco and food items.

Philip Morris, the US's leading food manufacturer, is also known to consumers as Kraft, General Foods, Miller Brewing Co., Oscar Mayer, and Oroweat, among others. Ten cents of every American food dollar is now spent on a Philip Morris product.

Conglomerate concentrations tend to have multiple contacts with one another, which blunts the edge of their competition, as any advantage gained in one market may be set off or be threatened by loss in another market. These giant corporations generally adopt a live-and-let-live policy towards one another.

Aggregate Concentration

This form of concentration, which is particularly evident in agribusiness, involves relationships between the conglomerates such as interlocking directorates, inter-corporate stock holdings, historical relationship, etc., that allow them to exist not just as corporate powers but also as influences of political power. Such concentration makes sure that the members 'toe the line'; it also reduces the potential for independent, competitive behaviour.

Concentration and Increasing Unemployment

Concentration in the food sector is not just achieved by organic growth where companies patiently build up market share by efficiencies or other means. In the 1990s, the food manufacturing sector was characterized by an extraordinary period of mergers and acquisitions both within national markets and across borders. Trade liberalization accelerates this process, creating a twin-track economy-large and small.

❑❑❑

5

Globalization of Agriculture

1. Diverse Seeds for Diversity

FARMERS FOR millennia have studied, identified, modified, cultivated and exchanged seeds freely in order that they may provide for themselves the best for their utilisation. In this capacity the farmer has always been a scientific plant breeder. Farmers have traditionally conserved and developed this diversity in their fields through on-going cultivation of the varieties. As the farmer produced mainly for the family, the village, and then the rest of the world, with the main vision being sustainability of both lifestyle, and nature (including land and water resources), it was in his interest to conserve the plant varieties developed by him.

Genetic diversity is essential in agriculture for developing plants with characteristics to suit the ecological conditions, nutritional needs and other uses by farmers and for conferring at least partial resistance to diseases. Therefore, it is important to understand biodiversity in its totality and not just in terms of food crops alone. There exists a symbiotic relationship in the ecological niche in which the crops grow. Diversity plays an important role in nutrient cycling, controlling insect population and plant disease. Thus, on-field conservation of all diverse plant wealth is imperative for sustainable agriculture.

Seeds of agricultural crops have been developed over centuries by farming communities across the world. These seeds have been freely exchanged with other communities again across the world and have led to the development of new varieties. Today, with the entry of the multinational sector in seed production and supply as well as new technologies for producing seed, seed varieties have been given a variety of names depending on who evolved it, how it was evolved and its potential for making profits.

Farmers' varieties are those varieties which have been developed by farmers over the years to suit their ecological, nutrition, taste, medicinal, fodder, fuel, and other needs. These have sometimes been called landraces to distance them from the contributions that farmers have made towards their evolution through selection. They have also derogatorily been called primitive cultivars in contrast to elite cultivars as those evolved by scientists. Farmers' varieties like any other seed variety, are an embodiment of intellectual contribution. Farmers' varieties are perennial and sustainable. Farmers' varieties are also referred to as indigenous seeds, native seeds, organic seeds, heirloom seeds and heritage seeds, jwaari, nate, desi etc.

High yield varieties (HYVs), or green revolution seeds are misnamed because the term implies that the seeds are high yielding. The distinguishing feature of these seeds, however, is that they are actually, *high response varieties*. Though these seeds can be saved by farmers, they are non-sustainable due to vulnerability to diseases and pests and therefore need to be replaced after one or two crops.

Hybrid seeds are the first generation seeds (F1) produced from crossing two genetically dissimilar parent species. The progeny of these seeds cannot economically be saved or replanted, as the next generations will give much lower yields.

Hybridisation is only one of the breeding techniques. It does provide high-yielding varieties, but so do other breeding techniques. It is thus like biological patenting the seed. No one else, neither the farmer nor a rival company, can produce exactly similar seeds unless they know the parent lines, which are the company's secrets. This characteristic of the hybrid seed has been fundamental to the rapid growth of the American Seed Industry. The corporate seed sector in India is also involved mainly in the development of hybrid seeds including seeds of maize, sorghum, vegetables and foodgrains.

The hybrid seeds are also called "Sarkari" seeds as these seeds have initially been developed and distributed by the public sector in India.

Today there are three kinds of producers of seeds :

(a) *Farmer Seeds* : The farmer has historically been the producer of perennial varieties, which could reproduce themselves eternally.

(b) *Public Sector Seeds* : Public sector research institutions have bred short term varieties for "high yield". These seeds could for some time be saved and used by the farmer, but their yield reduces after a few years.

(c) *Private Sector Seeds* : Private companies and Transnational corporations produce non-renewable and therefore non-sustainable seeds through hybrids and tissue culture, where the farmer has to return to the company for fresh seed, each time he has to sow.

The last is called biological patenting of seed. Patents give the owner of the seed the exclusive right to multiply, save, develop further varieties and sell seeds. Biological patenting effectively prevents the farmer from multiplying, saving and selling the seed.

2. The Decline of the Public Sector

The shift from indigenous varieties of seeds to the Green Revolution (high yielding and hybrid) varieties also involved a shift from a farming system controlled by peasants to one controlled by agri-chemical and seed corporations, and international agricultural research centres. The shift also implied that from being a free resource reproduced on the farm, seeds were transformed into a costly input to be purchased. Countries had to take international loans to diffuse the new seeds, and farmers had to take credit from banks to use them. International agricultural centres supplied, seeds, which were then reproduced, crossed and multiplied at the national level.

The National Seed Policy

The Royal Commission of Agriculture (est. in 1928) was the first body to recognise the necessity of the high quality seed. In seeking to promote the agriculture, Royal Commission placed emphasis on the production and distribution of the quality seed. The National Seed Corporation Ltd. (NSC) was founded in 1963 and was charged with the systematic production and distribution of seeds. This action was followed by the passage of Central Seed Act, which provided the statutory support for quality control. The National Seed Review Team was constituted in 1967 to make recommendations to the National Commission on Agriculture. Among the recommendations were strengthening the power of NSC and to foster the creation of additional government organisations to produce and distribute seed, including the State Farm Corporation of India (SFCI), 13 State Seed Corporations (SSCs), 19 seed certification agencies and 26 seed testing laboratories. The passage of Central Seed Act, 1996 laid the legal foundation for present-day seed industry. During the 1960s and the 1970s the participation of the private seed industry was minimal. The situation changed dramatically in mid-1980s, when the private seed industry experienced a sudden expansion; primarily by the appearance of the attractive market of hybrid sorghum and pearl millet. The specific policy reforms introduced in the 1987 further encouraged the growth of private seed industry. There was a subtle take over of the government control of the seed by the private companies. Firstly, many public breeding institutes began making germplasm (*e.g.* inbred lines) more readily available to private companies. Secondly, industry licensing policy was modified to attract greater participation of Indian companies as well as companies with minority foreign ownership.

The so-called reform process further threw open in 1988 with the passing of the New Policy for Seed Development. This landmark legislation was the process of handing over the seed sovereignty of the country to the foreign participation. The New Policy for Seed Development permitted private companies to import seed of vegetables, flowers and ornamental plants, although the imported material was subjected to prior approval by the Indian Council of Agricultural Research (ICAR). Imports of the seed of coarse cereals, pulses and oilseeds were also permitted following the approval from ICAR. In the seed production and distribution the private companies are reluctant to deposit the seed to the government agencies on the pretext that these might fall in the hands of their competitors.

Policy reforms introduced in the 1980s and 1990s led to lowering of many legal barriers, which was characterised by the rapid growth in the number of companies. The MNCs by arriving with lucrative job offers and better working conditions have in fact marginalised the public R&D centres of the country. The Public Sector Units (PSUs) have very little of the talent as most of the professionals have gone to the other side. Although the research component still persists, but this drain has led to the deterioration of the public breeding programme of the government.

Whilst the Green Revolution of the 1960s and '70s was orchestrated by the public sector, the so-called "Second Green Revolution", based upon new hybrid and genetic technologies, will be driven by the private sector. Accompanying this shift is a change in motivation from one based upon the common interest (however misguided this may have proven to be in practice) to one based upon corporate profit. Who, under this new regime, will pursue research in the public interest where this does not concur precisely with corporate interest? In this section, the decline of the public sector seed industry will be charted. The text section will examine the rise of the private sector.

The Privatisation of the Public Sector

Under Structural Adjustment Programmes (SAPs), investment in the public sector, and therefore the çompetitiveness of this, has fallen. Its role has now diminished to :

- *Provision of open pollinated seed.* The majority of seed distributed by State Seed Corporations is open pollinated. The market for open pollinated seed is expected to decline as pressure to use hybrid seed increases. But at present, SSC sales of Open Pollinated Varieties (OPVs) do little to compete directly with private sector sales (predominantly of hybrid seed). Successful public sector pearl millet hybrids represent an exception, to this generation. However, the area planted under pearl millet (denigrated as a 'coarse cereal') is falling nationally.

- *Sale of hybrid seed in crops for which there is little private sector interest.* Public sector bajra (pearl millet) hybrids are extolled as demonstrating the continued competitiveness of public sector research and development. However, the area of land planted under pearl millet is actually falling annually, as farmers turn to other, more commercial crops.
- *Erosion of the public sector market shares.* It is a professed aim of State Seed Corporations and Agriculture Departments to encourage the shift to increased use of hybrid seed; a market increasingly dominated by transnational companies (or national companies with tie-ups with foreign companies).
- *Production of parental lines.* Increasingly, the role of public sector research institutions is viewed as the production of parental lines to be given to private companies for further development.
- *Sale of private sector seed.* Seed from private sector companies, particularly maize and sunflower seed from transnational, comprises an important proportion of total seed distributed through some State Seed Corporations. This attracts Central and State Government subsidies, amounting to direct though unacknowleged, governmental support for the private sector.

The Structure of the Public Sector

The National Seeds Corporation

The National Seeds Corporation (NSC) was established in 1963, with the massive importation of new high yielding varieties. The NSC became the distribution arm of the public sector, responsible for the production and marketing of varieties bred at ICAR funded institutes and agricultural universities. Its role has since been largely superseded by the State Seed Corporations. However, it still grows seed, under contract to 7000 farmers, to compensate for shortfalls in seed production by the SSCs. The NSC is an important producer of vegetable seed, particularly open pollinated varieties of around 100 products, and about nine are hybrids. It is claimed that the NSC produces vegetable seed over an area of 900,000 hectares, by comparison to a total private sector production area of 1,500,000 hectares. Despite being (or perhaps because it is) such an important producer of vegetable seed, attempts were made by World Bank representatives to persuade the director of the NSC to cut back vegetable seed production. Whether or not the private sector can be entrusted with the pricing of vegetable seed in the absence of public sector competition in equivocal. Cabbage seed imported from Japan and sold by the National Seed Corporations for Rs. 6000 per kilogram is sold by a private company for Rs. 12-15,000 per kilogram. Meanwhile, the NSC has maintained a workforce of around 600 (comparable to its strength in the 1960s), the private seed company is paying recent graduates Rs. 2,500 (or US $ 70) per month.

State Seed Corporations

Thirteen State Seed Corporations were established in 1975, under World Bank funding. These largely took over public sector seed production from the NSC. They still comprise a highly important sector of the Indian seed industry, particularly with respect to open pollinated cereal varieties. The managing director of Andhra Pradesh SSC, for example, estimates that this provides some 75 per cent of the seed requirements of the state; 40 per cent of this seed is hybrid, much of it provided by the private sector.

The remainder of the seed supplied by the State Seed Corporation, in the case of Andhra Pradcsh (AP), is produced by some 6000 share-holding "cultivating farmers". Nuclear seed, developed in the public sector — by ICRISAT, ICAR and the Universities — is used in the production of breeder, foundation and certified seed. This is then processed at one of eighteen processing units in the State, and supplied to farmers.

Some SSCs are financially profitable. The AP-SSC, for example returned an 8 per cent dividend to shareholders last year. It seems however, that profitability is set to increase the threat from the private sector. This is not merely manifest as an encroachment upon the market share of SSCs.

Research and Development

All private sector representatives concur that the competitiveness of public sector varieties and hybrids is falling. The managing director of IML Seeds estimates that 90 per cent of maize, and virtually all sunflower seed now sold, are private sector hybrids (or varieties). Even State Seed Corporations are increasingly supplying private sector hybrids. Several contributory reasons are suggested for this :

1. The success of private-sector advertising campaigns.
2. Funding problems, both nationally, with higher education funding in crisis, and internationally (for example, withdrawal of international funding for ICRISAT in Hyderabad), leading to under investment in public sector research programmes.
3. Public sector bureaucracy.
4. The failure of poorly trained SSC staff to properly maintain public sector lines, which are given to SSCs for perpetuation.

This has led to a shift in the role of the public sector. Increasingly, public sector research establishments are seen as the providers of lines for further development and refinement by the private sector. These are made freely available to private sector breeders.

Paddy and wheat seed sales are still dominated by the public sector, although with increasing private sector interest in hybrid paddy, the public sector sales of this seems to diminish. Sales of public sector hybrids of pearl millet are also good, though (as mentioned above) there is comparatively little private sector competition for the market for hybrids of so-called 'coarse cereals', for which the area cropped nationally is falling annually.

Many smaller seed companies have used sales of public sector hybrids and varieties. Other new companies have used sales of these to maintain viability whilst developing their own hybrids. Examples are provided by J.K. Agri Genetics and IML Seeds, both of which entered the seed market in 1989, in the wake of the New Seed Policy (1988). Initially, both companies relied upon sales of public-sector varieties and hybrids, before launching their own research and development programmes. However, it is generally recognised that relying exclusively upon sales of public bred hybrids is difficult. Such hybrids are available to all small companies, and competition is stiff. Subsidies for public-sector suppliers of this seed makes private sector involvement less attractive. In response to the intensive advertising campaigns of large seed companies, farmers are moving increasingly towards use of proprietary hybrids. Many smaller seed companies will be hard-hit by the dual effects of the diminishing competitiveness of public-sector varieties and hybrids, and heavy investment in the expansion of the private sector market for proprietary hybrids.

World Bank Funding of the Public Sector

World Bank-funded National Seed Projects (NSP) were initiated in the mid-seventies, to make the Indian seed industry 'more viable and result-orientated'. That is, to create necessary infrastructural facilities for 'seed production, conditioning, storage and distribution of high quality seeds'. Three such Projects (NSP I, NSP II, and NSP III) were undertaken (beginning in 1975, 1981, 1988 respectively). The last of these three ran up until 1996.

TABLE 1

Proportion of World Bank funding for each successive National Seed Project earmarked for the private sector

National Seed Project	*Beginning (Year)*	*Apportioned to Private Sector (Approximate)*
NSP I	1975	—
NSP II	1981	20-25 per cent
NSP III	1988 (ran until 1996)	60 per cent

Source : *Personal communication by Tom Crompton with K.R. Chopra, World Bank Consultant, 1997.*

In particular, World Bank policy changed in 1993, when it was concluded that investment in the public sector seed industry was unproductive. Subsequently, support was concentrated in the private sector. In the case of NSP III US $ 30 million credit was made available to private companies through the National Bank for Agricultural and Rural Development (NABARD) under favourable loan agreements. Specifically, these were made available for infrastrucutral improvements, germplasm import, agricultural education and seed testing (they did not cover working capital or land purchase). Recently, an FAO team recommended against a Fourth Project, concluding that the growth of the seed industry will continue without further intervention. However, individual state governments are invited to submit applications for financial support for the private sector to the World Bank. Uttar Pradesh, where the private sector is 'under-developed', is pursuing such sources of funding.

3. The Privatisation of the Seed Sector

The Indian seed industry is undergoing a period of rapid change inaugurated by the economic liberalisation of the past decade including the New Seed Policy of 1998. The structural adjustment programmes of the 1990's and the coming into force of the W.T.O. agreements on Trade Related Intellectual Property Rights (TRIPs), the New Seed Policy lifted restrictions on private sector import of foreign germplasm, enabling larger seed producers, particularly those with foreign collaborations, to access seeds from international sources. Increasingly, the public and private sectors are being delineated in terms of the type of seed they each produce. The public sector focuses on the development and production of open pollinated varieties (OPVs), which are less commercially exploitable than hybrid seeds. The private sector concentrates upon these latter and more remunerative crops (such as vegetables). This is a polarisation, which is set to continue, particularly as pressure on farmers to switch to use of high yielding hybrids intensifies. Despite this polarisation, both the public and private sectors are engaged in initiatives to increase hybrid seed usage amongst those farmers currently using open pollinated varieties.

Predictions suggest that the Indian seed industry will be worth some 20 billion rupees (around US $ 600 million) annually by the turn of the century. Indeed, the former managing director of Monsanto, estimates that it will be worth 60 billion rupees (around US $ 2 billion). As the commercial value of seed sales grows, the proportion of these accounted for by the public sector is diminishing, with more farmers turning to high yielding hybrid seeds produced by private seed companies. Simultaneously, there will be a continued coalescence of the industry around a few key companies, most of which will either be subsidiaries of transnational companies, or otherwise have entered joint agreements with such companies. Representatives of large seed companies (and in some instances the directors of smaller companies) admit that the future for low-turnover domestic seed enterprises looks grim.

There is uncertainty over the actual current value of the seed industry, though it is anticipated that this stands at 12,000-16,000 million rupees per annum. Estimates placed the value of the industry (both public and private) at 10,000 million rupees back in 1994. According to one such estimate, the value of seed sales broke down by market sector as detailed in Table 2.

TABLE 2

Estimate value of various sectors of seed industry, as of 1994 figures

(*in million Rupees*)

Public Sector	4000
Private Sector	6000
Organised	3500
Large	2150
Small	1350
Unorganised	2500
Total	**10000**

Source : *Data compiled by Mallick (1995). The operational definitions of 'large' and 'organised' are not clear.*

This massive and continued growth is attributed to a shift in seed sales away from the public sector and towards the private sector, commensurate with an increasing demand for high-yielding hybrid seed. According to the president of the Seed Association of India, the commercial exploitation of hybrid vigour in recent years has been a crucial factor in phenomenal increase of private sector contribution to the total turnover. The managing director of Mahyco, estimates that the distribution of the market has shifted since 1994 (see Table 2). However, these figures are essentially speculative, and he was unclear how he defined a 'large' (or 'small') company.

Table 3 shows one projection for a breakdown of the growth of the seed industry, by crop type.

Estimates of the proportion of the market accounted for by hybrid seed sales (in terms of value, rather than volume) also vary but the suggestion by Mr. S.U. Baig (Director, Nath Seeds) that this stands at 70-75 per cent represents a consensus viewpoint. Baig also estimates that 25 per cent of the market is held by 15 or 16 companies (perhaps 10 per cent of all companies nationally). The former manager of Monsanto suggests that there are only 15-20 'sustainable' seed companies

TABLE 3

Breakdown of the growth of the seed industry

Crop	*1994*	*1997*	*2002*
Paddy	200	275	350
Wheat	220	325	450
Sorghum	75	90	115
Maize	65	70	90
Pearl millet	35	44	60
Sunflower	10	14	20
Mustard	8	12	15
Others	87	170	400
Volume	700	1000	1500
Value (Rs. million)	**10,000**	**15,000**	**30,000**

Source : *Kapoor and Sindhu, 1995.*

Note : Seed Industry growth projections (thousand tonnes). The bottom row also shows total projected sales of seed, in both public and private sectors.

in the country. He suggests that suppliers within the public-sector have "only survived this long due to ignorance of farmers".

The reduction in the public sector market share is difficult to document, for two reasons. Firstly, the seed production of State Seed Corporations, the main public sector suppliers of seed, continue to grow. What is not clear is whether this is growing in proportion to the expansion of the overall market. Secondly, State Seed Corporations themselves buy seed from the private sector (Andhra Pradesh State Seed Corporation, for example, buys some 25 per cent of its seed from the private sector). This means that an appreciable proportion of seed sales by this Corporation are, in actual fact, attributable to the private sector.

Expectations for the expansion of the seed market are derived from two considerations. The first is based upon estimates that at present a high proportion of seed is saved by farmers from year to year. This may be seed saved from commercially bought open pollinated varieties, or even second generation (F2) hybrid seed. In addition, a significant proportion of this seed is taken from local 'landraces'. It is anticipated that farmers will increasingly buy new seed each year, and where they are using landraces, will turn to alternative commercial varieties and hybrids. The second consideration is that farmers are expected to increasingly turn to more expensive hybrid seed in preference to open pollinated varieties.

Farmer Saved Seed

Estimates of the ratio of farmers who replant saved seed each year vary. The managing director of IML Seeds, estimates that nationally in 1990 around 10 per cent of farmers bought new seed annually, rising to 25 per cent in 1997. He claims that this is now set to increase 5-6% per annum. The general manager of ProAgro-PGS, estimates that overall use of 'quality seed' is 9.5 per cent. The eighth five-year plan (1991-96) set a target of a 6 per cent seed replacement ratio. The target for the ninth five-year plan (running to 2001) is 8 per cent. Most farmer saved seed is OP or local landrace. Open pollinated (OP) seed performs well for four to five generations, with minimal selection of plants each year. In addition, some hybrid seed is planted in the second or third generation (F2 and F3). Second generation maize seed for example, is used in preference to new OP seed, according to the managing director of IML.

Table 4 shows the amount of seed supplied by the industry for six crops, in 1994. Also shown is the estimated percentage that this represents of the total seed planted. This is calculated on the basis of average seed requirements per unit area of a particular crop. As might be anticipated, relatively little seed is bought for crops which are predominantly open pollinated (paddy and wheat). Other crops where hybrid seed is available, show higher proportions of supplied seed. In fact, the proportion of sunflower seed that is taken from suppliers is now probably higher (estimates suggest that around 95 per cent of sunflower seed planted is hybrid, and most of this will be rebought annually).

TABLE 4

Seed supplied (in tonnes) by the seed industry in 1994, for a range of crops, and estimates of the proportion

Crop	*Seed supplied (tonnes)*	*Seed supplied as percentage of seed planted (calculated on basis of total area under crop)*
Paddy	150,000	11.7%
Wheat	200,000	8.3%
Sorghum	45,000	25.9%
Maize	35,000	29.4%
Pearl millet	30,000	71.8%
Sunflower	7,000	43,0%

Source : *Chopra et al. 1995.*

The Agricultural Commissioner for Andhra Pradesh estimates that between 10 per cent and 30 per cent of cereal seed planted in the state annually is of local landrace varieties. In particular, use of landraces is concentrated in :

- areas of newly-cultivated land, which tend to be farmed by novice farmers unclear of the advantages of use of commercial seed
- areas where water shortage makes investment in commercial seed less attractive
- areas where credit for purchase of commercial seed, fertilisers and pesticides is difficult to secure
- areas where local landraces are preferred due to local taste preference.

The Shift Towards Hybrids

At the National Conference on Seeds, Agra (in 1993), targets were set for annual increases in the hybrid seed production (expressed as mass of seed) until 1997 (see Table 5).

It is estimated that total hybrids use has increased from 8 per cent (1994) to an estimated 25 per cent (1997) of seed annually planted. The director of Nath Seeds estimates current hybrid seed use as shown in Table 6.

TABLE 5

Yearwise hybrid seed production plan (1992-93 to 1996-97)

Crop	*Annual growth rate (%)*
Maize	17
Sorghum	6
Pearl millet	22
Sunflower	63
Castor	14

Source : *Chopra et al. (1995). 'Annual Growth Rate' refers to annual targeted proportional increase in hybrid seed sales.*

Notes : Yearwise hybrid seed production plan (1992-93 to 1996-97), according to National Conference on seeds, Agra 993.

TABLE 6

Current estimates of hybrid seed sown as a proportion of the total seed of the corresponding crop planted each year

Crop	*Hybrid Seed Planted as a Proportion of the Total*
Cotton	23%
Sorghum (kharif)	95%
Pearl millet	50%
Maize	75%

Source : *S.U. Baig, Director, Nath Seeds (1997).*

Factors contributing to this remarkable increase in hybrid seed use will be considered in some detail. Chopra identifies two such factors : (1) the development (by the private sector) of short-maturing hybrids; (2) the hiking of grain prices, making heavy investment in hybrid seed commercially viable for those farmers who can afford it. Note the maintenance of these grain prices is determined in part by seed suppliers (Cargill, for example, who are able to manipulate maize prices, also sell hybrid seed for planting). To these two further factors might be added; (3) an intensive advertising campaign conducted by seed companies, and augmented by government-funded projects to increase farmer's acceptance of hybrid seed; and (4) according to some industry representatives, the effects of farmer-to-farmer advocacy of hybrid use. The marketing manager of Cargill, for example adopts a strategy encouraging farmers themselves to become "Cargill spokespeople".

The hybrid seed market is reputedly, highly fickle; farmers' preferences for particular brands of seed change rapidly, reflecting in part the specific marketing success of individual companies, and favouring those with a broad product portfolio. This viewpoint is corroborated by the manager of one small seed retail company, who claims that in his experience it takes just two years for farmers to switch allegiance to a new HYV or hybrid. This frequently follows heavy promotion of particular brands. He cites, for example, the case of a Western Agri cotton hybrid which was heavily promoted through the distribution of free 50 gm seed packets to selected high-performing farmers, and provision for an attractive profit margin for seed retailers.

Public Sector Campaigns

Subsidised Seed

The State Seed Corporations (SSCs) have two stated aims, summarised in the strategy document produced by Andhra Pradesh SSC. The first is to provide 'high quality seed to farmers at reasonable prices, the second is to 'coordinate with the Department of Agriculture, Government of Andhra Pradesh, in accelerating the spread of hybrid/high yielding varieties of different crops for promoting increased agricultural production'. This latter aim is addressed through both the provision of seed at subsidy, and the supply of private sector produced seed. In fact, as discussed earlier, 25 per cent of the seed supplied by AP-SSC is bought from the private sector (mainly maize and sunflower — crops dominated by multinational companies). This is an evident source of embarrassment for Director General of the Indian Council of Agricultural Research (ICAR). He points out that the policy of individual SSCs is beyond the control of Central Government, and claims that instances of these buying seed from the private sector are exceptional.

Farmers' Seminars

During the kharif season, 1997, the Government of Andhra Pradesh organised a series of Statewide *karshaka Sadassus*, or farmers' seminars. These comprised a two-day exhibition of agricultural technologies, and a programme of seminars extolling the applications of these. It was anticipated that around 30,000 farmers, representing all neighbouring villages, would attend each of the 22 Karshaka Sadassus. In addition, the participation of private seed companies was invited, to 'exhibit agri-inputs and other related products'. The seminars, it was claimed, offered 'a good opportunity for exposing the latest technology in agriculture, and inputs available to farmers'.

State Agricultural Training

In Andhra Pradesh, the State Agriculture Commission has set up a network of Farmers' Training Centres, with one to each district. These organise training, both at the Centre, and through two-day training sessions in villages, for groups of 25 to 30 farmers. In addition, each district has several development and agriculture officers.

The Intensive Tribal Development Agency (ITDA)

In Andhra Pradesh, the State Seed Corporation supplies seed to two regional Intensive Tribal Development Agencies (based at Paderu and Utnoor), for distribution amongst tribal peoples, at large subsidies. The managing director of the AP-SSDC predicts that within 2-3 years, all residual use of local landraces by tribals will be eradicated.

In Utnoor District (350,000 people, around 80,000 families) soyabean seed, black, green and red gram, paddy, cotton and sorghum (jowar) seed is supplied at a subsidy. Some of these represent new commercial crops for tribals (soyabean, for example). Others (jowar) are already grown as important landraces. Under a scheme that was initiated in early 90's, seed was initially supplied at a 75 per cent subsidy. This has since been cut to a current 50 per cent subsidy (25 per cent subsidy is provided by the Andhra Pradesh Department of Agriculture, with the ITDA meeting the remainder). Under the scheme, fertilisers and pesticides are also provided at a subsidy, with the government providing subsidies on fertilisers, and the ITDA a 50 per cent subsidy on biopesticides.

Only around 20 per cent of families can be supplied with subsidised seed. These are selected at a local level by the Village Tribal Development Association. Although the ITDA hopes to do away with the subsidy in the near future, the Project Officer admits that amongst those two whom subsidised seed is no longer made available, very few are continuing to plant hybrid seed. This is attributed to the difficulty encountered by tribals in securing loans. In the past, tribals have been forced to default on bank loans following crop failure (HYVs and hybrids are particularly vulnerable to this as a result of the more stringent growing conditions).

The Project Officer also concedes that there has been an increase in patriarchal power following a shift toward planting of commercial crops. This follows a reduction in the importance of the role of women in harvesting these crops. In an attempt to redress the balance, grant aid is simultaneously being given to women's projects, to encourage alternative enterprises (cattle breeding, or small market-based projects, for example).

Private Sector Campaigns

The private sector is predominantly concerned with conversion of farmers currently relying upon open pollinated varieties. Except in the case of sunflower, where most seed planted is hybrid (estimates are that the proportion is as high as 95 per cent), the potential for expansion of the hybrid market is seen as large. The president of Shriram Bioseed Genetics, for example, summarises the attitudes of many industry representatives when he comments : "Only after farmers currently dependent upon OPVs switch to hybrids, can we foresee the development of commercial interest in farmers still relying upon landraces".

This emphasis upon market expansion means that many companies profess to concentrate upon a development of the market *per se*, rather than pushing their own particular hybrid brand. Multinational seed companies invest most extravagantly in the development of the hybrid seed market. Cargill for example, organised a series of 'field-days' and demonstration plots. The company has a team of 'field assistants' which have the sole job of visiting farmers and 'cold-selling'. Strategies also include mail-shots and newspaper advertisements. The marketing manager claims that the key to their sales strategy is a 'farmer advocacy' — encouraging farmer themselves to advocate Cargill seed.

Field-Days

Farmers are invited to the field of another farmer exhibiting uncommonly high yields of branded seed. These exemplary farmers may be singled out before the growing season, on the basis of their competence in previous seasons, and asked to grow the relevant branded seed. Alternatively, exemplary crops may be chosen at the end of each growing season from amongst a company's customers. Cargill adopts the latter approach, choosing around ten exemplary fields in Karnataka alone, and inviting between 200 and 300 farmers of each. Those farmers invited are not, by and large Cargill customers. ITC Zeneca adopts the alternative approach : Selected farmers are given ITC Zeneca seed to plant, alongside local varieties. At harvest time, up to 500 neighbouring farmers are invited to a 'farm-day'. Here the farmer relates his experience of growing the seed to other farmers, and Zeneca technical staff are on hand to back him up.

Cargill augment field-day with 'Intensive Customer Contract Programmes' (ICCPs), where Cargill staff gather together a group of farmers, and 'sit under a tree with a folio chart, to talk to them'. By the end of their first season of sales, Cargill staff had held perhaps 3000 such sessions, each attended by 20 to 30 farmers.

Sales Men

Although all Cargill seed is distributed through Rallies, the company has an extensive marketing network of its own. Each member of a seven person marketing team employs a further 10-15 temporary staff. These temporary staff are taken from farming communities local to those in which they will work. Cargill's marketing manager claims that this means sales staff appear 'more credible'.

Media

ITC Zeneca have a touring cinema which shows short film dramatising inter-village competition for the annual trophy for the best crop. The consistent victory of one village is attributed to its use of Zeneca seed. Following adoption of the same seed by the neighbouring village, both become equally successful, and the rival villagers are reconciled under the slogan 'with ITC Zeneca, it's a win-win situation'.

Cargill view their Krishi Kaipidi (or 'Farmer's Handbook') as a public-relations tool. This is published in fortnightly instalments in local newspapers during the growing season, and offers farmers practical advice on maximising the yields they obtain with their hybrid seed.

In engineering their dramatic (though self-proclaimed) rise to prominence as suppliers of maize seed in the north, Kanchan Ganga sold seed at a loss for the last two years, or so in order to establish a market. Cargill also may provide small packets of free seed to farmers, particularly poor farmers in areas where use of open pollinated varieties predominates. Cargill's marketing manager claims that free seed is not used as a strategy for converting farmers from rival brands of hybrid seed to Cargill seed.

4. Big Companies Getting Bigger

It is estimated that a total of 147 private sector seed companies, which can be broadly categorised according to whether they (1) develop, produce and market their own varieties and hybrids, (2) produce and market public sector varieties and hybrids, or (3) have no production capacity whatsoever, concentrating solely upon marketing. It is also estimated that of the former category, 24 companies have entered collaboration with foreign companies. In addition several multinational companies have opened subsidiaries in India.

There are several recent and discrete legislative changes which have promoted the growth of the private sector, which one identifies as follows :

1986 — Provision of private seed companies with breeder seeds for public sector developed self-pollinated crop varieties

1988 — New Seed Policy, liberalising seed imports and encouraging foreign investment in the sector

1991 — Relaxation of limitations on foreign participation, permitting foreign companies to hold controlling stakes in industrial enterprises.

The Market Niche of MNCs

Multinational Companies dominate in crops where access to international germplasm, places them at an advantage over national companies. In particular, these are maize, Sudan-grass/sorghum hybrid (SSG), cauliflower and soya. Rather than developing new hybrids specifically for use in India, multinational companies have tended to focus upon the exhaustive testing of extant hybrids imported from other countries, for suitability to Indian conditions. For example, Cargill maize and sunflower hybrids (which are 'price leader's' reflecting, it is claimed, their superior quality) were imported from international sources. Of the four biggest suppliers of sunflower seed, three (ITC Zeneca, ProAgro and Cargill) are multinational, reflecting the origin of all sunflower germplasm in the US.

Now, however, multinational companies are beginning to move into crops which have been dominated hitherto by domestic companies. Cargill, for example, are poised to push sales of sorghum hybrids.

Multinational companies have a characteristic sales strategy, typified by Cargill, preferring to emphasis 'quality' and consumer confidence, rather than competitive pricing. Thus Cargill's hybrid sunflower seeds retails for Rs. 350 per kilogram, over three times the price of hybrid sunflower seed produced by a local company, Bhavani Seeds (see Table 7). Cargill justifies this price on the basis of higher yield, consumer confidence, and after-sales back up. Besides, it is claimed, only 3-5 per cent of a farmer's total outlay cost is spent on seed. (Cargill claim that a progressive farmer spends perhaps 8 per cent of his cost of production on hybrid seed, but can achieve a 50 per cent yield advantage). The local seed company concedes that the yields obtained using Cargill seed exceed those obtained with its own proprietary hybrid. However, they suggest that the yield gains alone do not justify the vastly inflated prices. The production manager suggests that typical yields obtained with Cargill

TABLE 7

Cost of contract seed production, and retail prices, for three classes of sunflower seed (1997-98)

	Buys from Contract Grower (Rs./quintal)	*Retails to Customer (Rs./quintal)*
Bhavani Seeds Sunflower variety	20	40
Bhavani Seeds Sunflower hybrid	40-45	140
Cargill Sunflower hybrid	140	350

Source : *Figures quoted by production manager of Bhavani Seeds.*

sunflower seed would be 12-13 quintals per hectare, as compared to 10 quintals per hectare using Bhavani Seed's own hybrid. Cargill sales, he suggests, are maintained only through massive advertising campaigns with which smaller companies cannot hope to compete.

Case-Studies of Specific Markets

The Maize Market

The maize market is growing rapidly, and is expected to continue to grow as the processed food market expands under liberalisation. Calculated upon the basis of the total area nationally under maize, the potential seed market is reckoned to be some 120,000 tonnes. With Cargill (the price leader) selling maize seed for over US $ per kilogram, the maize market alone is viewed as being worth a potential US $ 120 million. Note that Cargill, the largest supplier of maize seed to the Indian market, also have some control over global grain prices, and hence the relative economic benefits to the farmer of investing in expensive hybrid seed. Cargill are attempting to force up the price of maize

TABLE 8

Trends in areas of maize planted, and amount of certified seed distributed, for the first half of the decade

Year	*Area of maize Plants (million hectares)*	*Certified seed distributed (tonnes)*
1990-91	5.90	14,900
1991-92	5.86	15,000
1992-93	5.96	15,000
1993-94	6.00	12,900
1994-95	6.11	13,700

Source : *Ram, 1996.*

(Note that whilst the area of maize planted has increased, on aggregate, over this period, the amount of certified seed supplied has fallen. This suggests a shift away from certified seed, towards private sector seed use.)

seed : The company sells the seed at three times the Indian price in Pakistan (US $ 3.50 per kg). This price differential is attributed to the lower domestic production of maize seed in Pakistan. Of course, diminishing domestic production of seed by domestic Indian companies will inevitably follow the consolidation of the multinational market share. The price of maize seed, it seems, is set to increase.

It is clear that the area planted under maize is increasing annually, whilst sales of certified seed is falling (Ram, 1996) (see Table 8). If we assume that the proportion of farmer's saved seed is also falling from year to year, it is evident that an increasing fraction of maize seed planted, though bought commercially, is not certified. This in turn suggests a shift from public sector (generally certified) to private sector (usually uncertified) seed usage.

The director of Pioneer estimates that around 90 per cent of the maize market is in the private sector. Some estimates suggest that currently, 25 per cent of maize seed planted annually is hybrid (25-30,000 tonnes of seed), around 60 per cent of open pollinated variety, and 15 per cent landrace. However, it is considered difficult to differentiate clearly between the OP and landrace share of the market. Landraces are used particularly in the north of India, in the Indo-Gangetic belt. Here cropping patterns demand a short-maturing maize. Whereas local landrace mature in 60-70 days, the quickest maturing hybrid requires 85-90 days. Although yields may be down, maize is grown principally for domestic (as opposed to commercial) use; maturation time is prioritised over yield. The marketing manager of Cargill estimates that over half the country's maize is grown in the north, with landraces accounting for perhaps two thirds of this (note an inconsistency here with the estimate that 15 per cent of maize planted nationally is landrace). By comparison, in the south maize is grown as a commercial crop and hybrids predominate in Karnataka, for example, it is estimated that 70-80 per cent of maize is hybrid.

Initiatives are being taken by seed companies to develop the market for hybrid maize in the north. Ultimately, it is believed that the full market potential will be realized only when short-maturing, high-yielding hybrids become available. Kanchan Ganga Seeds claim to have developed such a hybrid, which has seen their maize seed sales leap from 5 tonnes in 1995 to 1,300 tonnes in the first half alone of 1997. Such examples of the direct targeting of hybrid seed at farmers who currently rely upon landraces is uncommon, at least at present. However, in this instance, many of the farmers sowing local landrace varieties of maize are simultaneously using propriety hybrid seed in other crops.

The alternative approach is to encourage the planting of maize as a commercial crop in the north. Cargill have entered an agreement with Anil Starch, which has a production unit in Ahmedabad requiring large quantities of maize. Under the agreement, Anil guaranteed to buy Cargill maize from nearby Rajasthan farmers, dramatically boosting Cargill sales in the State.

Sorghum Market

It is estimated that the total area under sorghum is in the region of 12 million hectares, of which approximately 3.5 million hectares is under (accounting for annual hybrid seed sales of around 25,000 tonnes). Most of the remaining 8.5 million hectares is thought to be under landraces, with sales of OP sorghum low. There are two important sorghum seasons, *kharif* (autumn) and *rabi* (spring). 95 per cent of sorghum seed planted in the kharif season is hybrid. This is used principally for fodder. The rabi crop is planted for domestic use (human consumption) and relies upon local landraces, which are tastier, and which are more resistant to the shoot fly than proprietary plants.

Hitherto, private companies have had difficulty entering the sorghum market, particularly for the rabi planting. This is for several reasons :

1. The yield benefits of hybrids over open pollinated varieties are low;

2. Sorghum flour is used for making rotis, and farmer's preferences lie firmly with the taste of local varieties;
3. Public-sector seed is good and of course, cheaper.

Despite this increasing interest in rain-fed crops, hybrid coarse cereals are sold mainly in assured rainfall areas. In areas where rainfall cannot be assured, farmers are reluctant to invest heavily in expensive seed and the additional inputs required for cultivation of hybrids. Company representatives recognise the market potential for low-input intensive hybrids in areas where rainfall is not assured, but cannot foresee the development of this in the near future.

The Vegetable Market

The market in seed of temperate vegetables far pre-dates the green revolution. However, the first hybrid vegetable seeds were introduced much later than cereals, with the release by Indo-American (which, despite its name, is wholy an Indian company) of tomato and capsicum hybrids in the mid 70's. Hybrids purportedly extend the possible cropping season, offer improved disease resistance, uniformity of size, and improved transportability. Table 9 lists estimated proportions of hybrid vegetable in total cropped area for the year 1993-94. These

TABLE 9

Estimated proportions of hybrid vegetable in total cropped area for the year 1993-94

Crop	*Proportions of hybrids*
Brinjal	4.03
Cabbage	21.14
Cauliflower	0.59
Chillies	0.45
Gourds	1.18
Melons	2.10
Okra	0.77
Tomato	24.22

Source : *Arora, 1995.*

national figures obscure more dramatic adoption of hybrid seed in some state. The managing director of Century Seeds, writes that "there has been 100 per cent replacement of open-pollinated varieties with hybrids in major parts of Karnataka, Tamil Nadu, Maharashtra and West Bengal" (Arora, 1995).

According to Arora, public sector institutions have been handicapped by poor seed distribution networks, and have tended to focus upon lower value crops like okra and peas. He claims that 'their [the public sector's] mindset is still not turned to the high risk involved in demand/supply uncertainties and sudden varietal obsolescence. Private hybrids are spreading at a much faster pace'.

Opportunities for multinational companies in the Indian vegetable seed market are different from those in cereals. In the case of the latter, foreign companies can rely upon selling hybrids developed elsewhere, but found to the appropriate to the Indian market (take Cargill, for example, which spent two years checking existing hybrids for suitability to the Indian climate and market). In the case of vegetable seed production, however, greater adaptation of extant hybrids is needed in order to tap the Indian market. In practice, this means that multinational companies (like Peto and SVS Seminis) is then relied upon as the basis for development of hybrid suited to the Indian market.

Response of National Seed Companies to MNCs

Representatives of large Indian seed companies (for example, Nath, Mahendra, Mahyco, Indo-American) identify several areas where competition from multinational companies will not greatly impinge on their own market shares. Firstly in the case of cereals, they do not foresee serious competition from MNCs in the sale of sorghum or pearl millet, for which access to international sources of germplasm is of little value. Secondly, it is felt that, even where the hybrids offered by multinational companies are accepted as good (principally, maize and sunflower) these companies simply do not have the marketing base, production infrastructure of distribution system to capitalise upon this. These expectations may be ill founded, or simply affected. The managing director of Mahendra seeds reports with a note of optimism that multinational companies 'only' have half the maize market. He goes on to say 'the widespread fears of the effects upon domestic companies of the Seeds Policy of 1998 and the opportunities this has opened up for multinational companies have proven ill-founded'. But with half of maize seed sales, according to his own estimates, going to multinational companies, can he really be so complacent?

The president of Indo-American Hybrid Seeds is more candid in his criticism of multinational companies. He has seen the market share of Indo-American seeds decline since 1998, and is bitter about the aggressive marketing policies of multinational companies, 'with the investment potential to support low pricing'. Indo-American Seeds had also lost key staff to multinational companies. Attavar's response has been to look for tie-ups with foreign companies. Seminis Seed, for example, is produced and sold by Indo-American, and capsicum seed grown and exported for Peto. Indo-American has recently completed a huge capsicum seed production facility at Bangalore. This comprises one hundred greenhouse, each 40 meters by 10 meters, with a total capacity of 18 kg of seed per greenhouses. In a celebration of a showcase of Indian industry, the site was opened by the then Prime Minister, Deve Gowda. There is some irony to the fact that the unit is in fact used for the contractual production and export of capsicum seed for a large multinational.

Indo-American is not the only large Indian private seed company to have seen its market share eroded following multinational competition. Mahyco, for example, enjoyed an 85 per cent share of the market for sunflower seed in 1988. Today, their share (of an albeit expanding market) has fallen to just 10 per cent. This is attributed by multinational company representatives to poor genetic practice, and careless seed production.

It seems clear that, at least for the immediate future, the size of the Indian seed market is set to increase dramatically. Whilst this growth is sustained, direct competition between seed companies may be averted. It is generally accepted that competition between companies will intensify.

Small Companies

The managing directors of several small Indian seed companies are evidently very concerned to form collaborative linkages with foreign companies. One, having solicited a member of Research Team to look for potential UK collaborators, remarked melodramatically 'we must join hands with them [foreign companies] or die'. Whilst this director has tried out fifty or more varieties of foreign seed, in the hope of interesting companies with successful hybrids in a joint venture, none took him up. Despite his own difficulty in finding a foreign collaborator, he foresees increased collaboration between smaller Indian seed companies and MNCs, 'after companies like Mahyco and ProAgro have all been taken'. Smaller companies will, he feels, fulfil a role in the distribution of new varieties, and possibly in the provision of Indian germplasm. Furthermore, smaller companies (and certainly Indian companies generally) are allegedly more aware of the importance of appeasing middlemen in the distribution chain. In some instances, seed passes through three such middlemen between producer and customer (a distributor, a dealer, and a retailer). Whereas multinational of Bejo Sheetal, claims that it is these middlemen who really establish sales. Consequently, it is important, he claims, to provide these with appreciable margins. The director of Nath Seeds also recognises the importance of the role of dealers, claiming 'farmers blindly follow dealers'.

In addition, some foresee a continued market for cheaper open-pollinated seed varieties. Those poorer farmers who cannot afford hybrid seed, or higher input levels, and are vulnerable to increase in the prices of fertilisers and pesticides, are seen to present a secure market for small domestic companies. It is also claimed that these farmers are becoming increasingly aware of the accumulative and deleterious effects of saving seed from open pollinated varieties from year-to-year. Contamination from neighbouring crops leads, it is suggested, to a diminution in yield. Such farmers are therefore increasingly rebuying open pollinated seed on an annual basis.

Small companies also hope from their conviction that open pollinated varieties have a longer projected marketable life expectancy. Hybrid varieties derived principally from Western germplasm are, it is claimed by representatives of companies speciallising in open pollinated varieties, more susceptible to pests and diseases. Indeed, most company representatives admit that hybrid seed has a commercial longevity of around five years.

Hybrid seed use represents a higher risk, which many farmers are not prepared to take. However, that some MNC representatives specifically identify poorer farmers with smaller holdings as being those who could benefit most clearly from a switch to hybrid seed. Such a shift would, they claim, maximise the yields, and therefore profits, of smaller holdings. That many poorer farmers have not switched to hybrids is attributed, they claim, to a caution born out of ignorance, and to the difficulty experienced by small farmers in securing bank-loans. In the case of tomato for example, hybrid seed may be ten times more expensive than open pollinated seed (in terms of price per seeded acre). So, for example, open pollinated tomato seed sells for perhaps Rs. 300 per kilogram (sowing between 500 grams and one kilogram per acre). Hybrid seed sells for up to Rs. 50,000 per kilogram (sowing perhaps 40 grams per acre).

One alternative role for smaller seed companies is the contractual production of seed for larger companies (Sandoz, for example, contracts out seed production to smaller domestic companies). Unicorn Agrotech Ltd. is one such seed producer. This company concentrates mainly upon the production of seed for foreign companies, under contract. The managing director claims that there are perhaps five other similar companies which focus upon contract seed production, and there are still others which would like to move into this area.

6

Biological and Intellectual Heritage Protection

1. Protecting our Biological and Intellectual Heritage

THERE ARE two paradigms of biodiversity conservation. The first is held by communities whose survival and sustenance is linked to local biodiversity utilisation and conservation. The second is held by commercial interests whose profits are linked to utilisation of global biodiversity for production of inputs into large-scale homogenous, uniform, centralised and global production systems. For local indigenous communities, conserving biodiversity means to conserve the integrity of ecosystems and species, the right to these resources and knowledge, and their production systems based on biodiversity. For them, biodiversity has intrinsic value as well as high use value. For commercial interest, biodiversity itself has no value; it is merely 'raw material' for the production of commodities and for the maximisation of profits.

Most people in India even today live in the first paradigm of biodiversity utilisation. According to an ethnobotanical survey, there are 7,500 species used as medicinal plants by the indigenous medical traditions of India. These traditions are kept alive by 3,60,470 Ayurveda practitioners, 29,701 Unani experts and 11,644 specialists of Siddha. In addition, millions of house-wives, birth attendant and herbal healers carry on village-based health traditions. Seventy per cent healthcare needs in India are still met by traditional systems based on the use of medicinal plants.

Eight per cent of seeds used by farmers' seed supply, India is thus still a predominantly biodiversity-based economy.

The utilisation of biodiversity in people's economy is guided by a plurality of knowledge systems. The implementation of the properties, characteristics and uses of this biodiversity is held by local communities different languages, and in their diverse epistemological frameworks.

Nature's diversity and the diversity of knowledge systems is however undergoing a major process of destabilisation with the expansion of patents and intellectual property right into the domain of biodiversity via the TRIPs Agreement of the World Trade Organisation. TRIPs has been shaped by the objectives and interests of trade and transactional corporations (TNCs). It is totally inadequate for the objectives of protection and conservation of biodiversity.

The Convention on Biological Diversity (CBD) recognises that traditional knowledge, innovations and practices are of importance to the conservation of biological and that indigenous and local communities have a close and traditional dependence on biological resources. Their livelihood and life styles often depend on it and is shaped as it. As such in accordance to Article 10(c), Contracting Parties are obliged to protect and encourage customary use of biological resources in accordance with traditional cultural practices to conserve and sustainable use of these resources. Further, according to Art. 18.4 the Contracting Parties are also obliged to develop and use indigenous and traditional technologies to conserve biological diversity and sustainably use its components.

Changes in policy and law are being under these conflicting objectives of international treaties with respect to our biological heritage. The three most significant legal changes are :

(a) Amendments to the Indian Patents Act, 1970

(b) Introduction of Plant Variety legislation

(c) Introduction of a legal framework for biodiversity conservation.

While all these legislations have an impact on biodiversity and on our indigenous knowledge systems, there has so far not been an overall guiding framework to bring harmony and coherence into these laws on the basis of a balance between private and public interest, and conservation and utilisation objectives. While patent law changes are being introduced by the Agriculture Ministry and the biodiversity legislation is being introduced by the Environment Ministry.

No ministry is addressing the unique problems associated with the objective of conservation of medicinal plant biodiversity and the protection of indigenous systems of medicine and their practitioners, especially in the context of TRIPs. Article 27.5(3) of the TRIPs agreement states : parties shall provide for the protection of plant varieties either by patents or by an effective *sui generis* systems or by any combination thereof.

Since neither 'plant varieties' nor *sui generis* has been defined, countries free to interpret plant varieties as all plants and *sur generis* as a system uniquely adapted to the biodiversity endowment and knowledge heritage of the country. The Plant Variety Act drafted by the Agriculture Ministry to fulfil the *sui generis* option in fact defines plant and variety in a way they could cover medicinal plants. However, the Act is only aimed at seed and agricultural crops. It would be better to have one umbrella legislation for plant biodiversity, with one part of covering agriculture and farmers' rights and implemented jointly by the Agriculture Ministry and the Environment Ministry and the other part covering medicinal plants and indigenous health practitioners' rights, and implemented jointly by the Health Ministry and Environment Ministry.

Patents as currently defined on the basis of criteria of novelty, non-obviousness and industrial application, and 'invention' premised on reductionist criteria of chemical or genetic structures of plant and biological organisms, fail to recognise and give protection to indigenous knowledge traditions which have evolved over time, and which have different epistemological foundations than the western allopathic traditions based on a chemical paradigm.

Either the patent regimes need to be radically redefined to recognise collective innovation over time or new concepts for legal protection of biodiversity and indigenous knowledge need to be evolved. The need of evolving such as *sui generis* systems is an obligation of the Government as asignatory of the Biodiversity Convention.

If scientifically interpreted, the *sui generis* option in GATT can also be used to evolve legislation that covers medicinal plants and agricultural crops. Quite clearly, UPOV would be totally inadequate to this task of protecting medicinal plant biodiversity and the rights of practitioners of indigenous medical systems who use that biodiversity, since it is designed for agricultural crops and for the rights of industrial seed breeders. In any case, nowhere in the TRIPs agreement is mentioned that a *sui generis* system has to be UPOV.

The need for coherence of property rights regimes is also required by the Biodiversity Convention. According to Article 3 of the Convention, biological diversity will be treated as the sovereign property of the country of origin.

While so far sovereign control over natural resources was usually interpreted as state control, under the new political climate of decentralisation through the 73rd Amendment of the Constitution as well as liberalisation, it becomes necessary to define biodiversity property rights through the sovereign rights of local communities and traditional practitioners.

These sovereign biodiversity property rights, embodying both biological and intellectual heritage have to be formalised and protected as existing prior to intellectual property rights. The latter can exist only where they do not infringe on the former, otherwise it is infringement and violation of sovereignty.

2. From Pluralism to an Hierarchy of Knowledge Systems

Diversity and pluralism are the characteristics of the Indian environment and Indian society. We have a rich biodiversity of plants for food and medicine. This agricultural diversity and diversity of medicinal plants have in turn given rise to a rich plurality of knowledge systems in agriculture and medicine.

However, under the colonial influence our biological and intellectual heritage was devalued. The priorities of scientific development and R&D efforts guided by a western bias transformed the plurality of knowledge systems into an hierarchy of knowledge systems.

Hierarchy of knowledge systems — only reductionist methods of western science treated valid

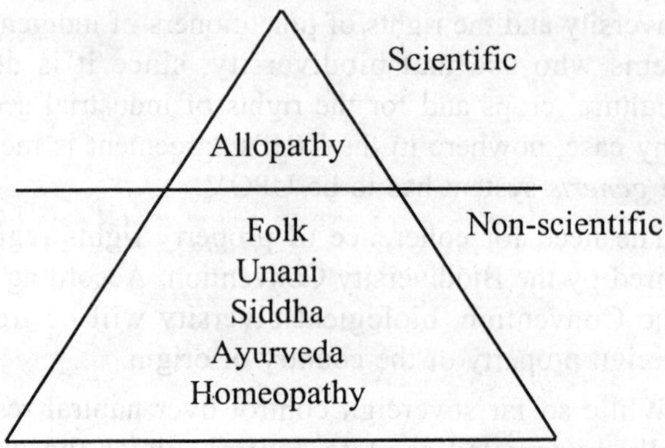

Fig. 1.

With knowledge plurality mutating into knowledge heirarchy, a horizontal ordering of diverse but equally valid and diverse systems is converted into a vertical ordering of unequal systems, with the epistemological foundations to the systems being imposed on others to invalidate them.

Western systems of knowledge in agriculture and medicine were defined as the only scientific system. Indigenous systems of knowledge were defined as inferior, and in fact as unscientific. Thus, instead of strengthening research on safe and sustainable plant-based pesticides such as neem and pongamia, we focused exclusively on the development and promotion of hazardous and non-sustainable chemical pesticides as D.D.T. and Sevin. The use of D.D.T. causes millions of deaths each year and has increased the occurrence of pests 12,000-fold. The manufacture of Sevin at the Union Carbide Plant in Bhopal led to the disaster which killed thousands and has disabled more than 4,00,000 people.

Meantime, as a recognition of the ecological failure of the chemical route to pest control, the use of plant-based pesticides is becoming popular in the industrialised world. Corporations that have promoted the use of chemical are now looking for biological options. In the search for new markets and control over the biodiversity base for the production of biopesticides, chemicals, TNCs like W.R. Grace are claiming IPRs on neem-based biopesticides.

The experience with agri-chemicals is replicated in the field of drugs and medicines. Indigenous systems of medicine and the biodiversity of medicinal plants were totally neglected in our scientific research and health policy which focused exclusively on the western allopathic systems and on technology transfer from the western pharmaceutical industry. Thus the health and pharmaceutical budget was heavily weighted in favour of the development and dissemination of the western allopathic systems. In spite of lack of official support, indigenous medical systems are based on over 7,000 species of medicinal plants and on 15,000 medicines of herbal formulations in different systems. The Ayurvedic texts refer to 1,400 plants, Unani texts to 342 and Siddha system to 328. Homeopathy uses 570, of which approximately 100 are Indian plants.

The economic value of medicinal plants to 100 million rural households is unmeasurable. Meantime, as a result to the increasing public awareness of side-effects of hazardous drugs, and the rise of strains resistant to antibiotics, the western pharmaceutical industry is increasingly turning to the plant-based system of India and Chinese medicine. Patenting of drugs derived from indigenous systems of medicine has started. The current value of the world market for medicinal plants from leads given by indigenous local communities is estimated to be US $ 43 billion.

Using traditional knowledge increased the efficiency of screening plants for medical properties by more than 400 per cent.

The failures and non-susceptibility of the chemical route to agriculture and health care provides an opportunity to re-evaluate knowledge systems, and move from the false hierarchy of these systems to a plurality. Such a pluralistic view of knowledge systems would imply respect for the different systems in their own logic and in their own epistemological foundations. It would also mean that one system (*viz.* the western) does not have to serve as the measure of scientific adequacy for all systems, and diverse systems do not need to be reduced to the language and logic of western knowledge systems. The integrity of our biological intellectual heritage can be protected only in such a pluralistic perspective. An hierarchical perspective will continue to project the western paradigm as scientifically superior in spite of its current failures in the context of susceptibility of health care and nutrition. The assumption of hierarchy is also the underlying basis for legitimising piracy as invention.

The phenomena of 'biopiracy' and 'intellectual piracy' in which western commercial interests claim products and innovations derived from and currently used by indigenous knowledge traditions as their 'intellectual property' protected through 'intellectual property rights' like patents has emerged as a result of the devaluation and hence the invisibility of indigenous systems to knowledge and the lack of protection for these systems. This devaluation is linked to the imposition of the reductionist methods of western science to the non-reductionist approaches of indigenous knowledge systems. Further since western style IPR systems are biased towards western knowledge systems which reduce biodiversity to its chemical or genetic structures, the indigenous systems get no protection, but piracy of these systems is protected.

In the absence of a protection systems for biodiversity and indigenous knowledge systems, and with the universalisation of western style IPR regimes, such intellectual and biological piracy will grow.

Protecting our biological and intellectual heritage in the age of biopiracy requires the recognition and rejuvenation of our heritage, and the evolution of legal systems for the protection of this heritage in context of emerging IPR regimes.

3. Biological and Intellectual Piracy

While the IPR debate during the Uruguay Round of GATT negotiations was framed on the grounds the stricter, western style IPR regimes were needed globally to prevent piracy by the South, in recent years it has become evident that the piracy is in fact being undertaken by corporations of the North which are appropriating the biodiversity and indigenous knowledge about it from the South. The issue of IPRs is thus getting closely related to the issue of biopiracy and intellectual piracy of western style IPR regimes. The lack of legal protection for our biological and cultural heritage has made the indigenous communities of the Third World vulnerable to 'biopiracy' and 'intellectual piracy' as illustrated by the cases of patents for products from Phyllanthus niruri and the Neem.

Western allopathic systems have no medical cure for jaundice or viral hepatitis. Jaundice in medical terms is basically the presence of certain signs and symptoms associated with liver dysfunction, *e.g.* yellowness of eyes, nausea, loss of appetite, pain in the liverregion etc. Indian systems of medicine — Ayurveda, Unani and Siddha — and folk traditions have used various plants for the treatment of jaundice. *Phyllanthus niruri* is one such medicinal plant used widely in India from north to south, from east to west. It is as much a part of formal health care system of Ayurveda as part of local health practices, folk medicine and traditional indigenous collective knowledge. The plant is called *Bhudhari* in Sanskrit, *Jar amla* in Hindi and *Bhuin amla* in Bengali.

Even though the use of *P. niruri* for treatment of jaundice has been an ancient and well recorded innovation in the Indian systems of medicine, patents are now being applied for this knowledge as if was a novel invention.

Neem, or *Azadirachta Indica*, has been used for diverse purposes over centuries in India. It has been used in medicine and in agriculture. Research has shown that neem extracts can influence nearly 200 species of insects, many of which are resistant to pesticides.

Several extracts of neem have recently been patented by US companies, and many farmers are incensed at what they regard as intellectual piracy. The village neem tree has become a symbol of Indian indigenous knowledge, and of resistance against companies, which seek to expropriate this knowledge for their own profit.

In the last 70 years, there has been considerable research upon the properties of neem carried on in institutes ranging from the Indian Agricultural Research Institute and the Malaria Research Centre to the T.E.R.I. and the Khadi and Village Industries Commission (KVIC). Much of this research was fostered by Gandhian movements such as the Boycott of Foreign Goods movement, which encouraged the development and manufacture of local Indian products. A number of neem based commercial products, including pesticides, medicines and cosmetics, have come in the market in recent years, some of them produced are in the small-scale sector under the banner of the KIVC, others by medium-size laboratories. However, there has been no attempt to acquire proprietary ownership of formulae, since, under Indian law, agricultural and medicine products are not patentable.

For centuries the Western World ignored the neem tree and its properties; the practices of Indian peasants and doctors were not deemed worthy of attention by the majority of British, French and Portuguese colonialists. However, in the last few years, growing opposition to chemical products in the West in particular to pesticides, has led to a sudden enthusiasm for the pharmaceutical properties of neem. In 1971, US timber importer Robert Larson observed the tree's usefulness in India and began importing neem seeds to his company headquarters in Wisconsin. Over the next decade he conducted safety and performance tests upon a pesticide neem extract called Margosan-O and in 1985 received clearance forth product from the US Environmental Protection Agency (EPA). Three years later he sold the patent for the product to the multinational chemical corporation, WR Grace and Company.

Since 1985, over dozen US patents have been taken out by US and Japanese firms on formulae for stable neem-based solution and emulsion and even for a neem-based toothpaste. At least four of the patents are owned by WR Grace, three by another US company, the Native Plan Institute, and two by the Japanese Terumo Corporation. Having garnerec their patents and with the prospect of a licence form the EPA. Grace has set about manufacturing and commercialising their product by establishing a base in India. The company approached several Indian manufacturers with proposals to buy up their technology or to convince them to stop producing value-added products and instead supply the company with raw material.

In many cases, Grace met with a rebuff. M.N. Sukhatme, Director of Herringer Bright Chemicals Pvt. Ltd. which manufactures the neem-based insecticide Indiara, was put under pressure by Grace to sell the technology for a storage-stable neem extract which does not require heating or any chemical change. Sukhatme refused their offers. Eventually W.R. Grace managed to arrange a joint venture with a firm called P.J. Margo Pvt. Ltd. They have set up a plant in India which processes up to 20 tons of seed a day. They are also setting up a network of neem seed suppliers, to ensure a constant supply of the seeds at a reliable price. Grace is likely to be followed by other patent-holding companies.

In 1992, the US National Research Council published a report designed to 'open up the Western world's corporate eyes to the seemingly endless variety of products the tree might offer'. According to one of the members of the NRC panel, 'In this day and age, when were not very happy about synthetic pesticides, neem has great appeal'.

This appeal is blatantly commercial. This US pesticides market is worth about US $ 2 billion. At the moment biopesticides such as pyrethrum, together with their synthetic mimics, constitute about US $ 450 million of this, but that figure is expected to rise to over US $ 800 million by 1998. 'Squeezing bucks out of the neem ought to be relatively easy' observes *Science* magazine.

Grace's aggressive interest in Indian neem production has provoked a chorus of objections from Indian scientists, farmers and political activists, who assert that multinational companies have no right to expropriate the fruit of centuries of indigenous experimentation and several decades of Indian scientific research. This has stimulated a bitter transcontinental debate about the ethics of intellectual property and patent rights. In April 1993, a Congressional Research Service (CRS) report to US Congress out some of the arguments used to justify patenting.

Azadirachtin itself is a natural product found in the seeds of the neem tree and it is the significant active component. There is no patent on it. Perhaps because everyone recognises it as a product of nature. But...asynthetic form of a naturally occurring compound may be patentable, because the synthetic form is not technically a product of nature, and the process by which the compound is synthesised may be patentable.

However, neither *azadirachtin*, a relatively complex chemical, nor any of the other active principles have yet been synthesised in laboratories. The existing patents apply only to methods of extracting the natural chemical in the form of a stable emulsion or solution, methods which are simply an extension of the traditional processes used for millennia for making neem-based products. The biologically active polar chemicals can be extracted using technology already available to villages in developing countries, says Eugene. Schultz, chair of the NRC panel.

W.R. Grace's justification for patents, therefore, pivots on the chain that these modernised extraction processes constitute a genuine innovation :

> Although traditional knowledge inspired the research and development that led to these patented compositions and processes, they were considered sufficiently novel and different from the original product of nature and the traditional method of use to be patentable.

In short, the processes are supposedly novel and an advance on Indian techniques. However, this novelty exists mainly in the context of the ignorance of the West. Over the 2,000 years that neem-based biopesticides and medicines have been used in India, many complex processes were development to make them available for specific use, though the active ingredients were not given Latinised 'scientific' names. Common knowledge and common use of neem was one of the primary reasons given by the Indian Central Insecticide Board for not registering neem products under the Insecticides Act, 1968. The Board argued that neem materials had been in extensive use in India for various purposes since time immemorial, without any known deleterious effects. The US EPA, on the other hand, does not accept the validity of traditional knowledge and imposed a full series of safety tests upon *Margosan*.

P.J. Margo, Grace's Indian partner claim : *Azadirachtin*, which was being destroyed during conventional processing of Neem Oil/New Cake is being additionally extracted in the form of water-soluble neem extract and hence it is an add-on rather than a substitute to the current neem industry in India.

The allegation that *azadirachtin* was being destroyed during traditional processing is inaccurate. The extracts were subject to degradation, but this was not a problem since farmers put such extracts to use as and when they needed them. The problem of stabilisation arose only when it needed to be packaged for a long time to be marketed commercially.

Moreover stabilisation and other advances attributable to modern laboratory technology, had already been developed by

Indian scientists in the 1960s and 1970s, well before US and Japanese companies expressed interest in them.

Margosan-O is a simple ethanolic extract of neem seed kernel. In the late sixties we discovered the potency of not only ethanolic extract, but also other extracts of neem.... Work on the neem as pesticide originated from this division as early as 1962. Extraction techniques were also developed in a couple of years.

The reluctance of Indian scientists to patent their inventions, that leaving their work vulnerable to piracy, may in part derive from recognition that the bulk of the work had already been accomplished by generations of anonymous experimenters. This debt has yet to be acknowledged by the US patentors and their apologists. The CRS repay claims that the method of scattering ground neem seeds as a pesticide would not be a patentable process, because this process...would be deemed obvious — a statement that betrays either lamentable misjudgment or a racist dismissal of indigenous knowledge. The discovery of neem pesticidal properties and of how to process it was by no means 'obvious but evolved through extended systematic knowledge development'.

Two of the neem patents held by W.R. Grace have been challenged one in the US and one in the European Patent Office with the objective of highlighting the issue of biopiracy and the need to create legal system that take full cognizance of the innovation which has given rise to indigenous systems of knowledge and treat development built on this knowledge. For example in the case of U.S. Patent No. 5,124,349, the process described the W.R. Grace, to effect stable formulations, were known at the time of patenting. As one reviewer of the patent commented 'I find it incomprehensible that W.R. Grace could have been granted patent...claiming novelty on a process the whole world has known for years.'

Solvents mentioned in the patent and solvents similar to them have been used on neem seeds and described in publications before the company's application.

The main reason why such obvious steps are treated as novel is that the basic knowledge exists non-western traditions and therefore not known to the patent offices in the west. While the knowledge of indigenous systems is used, it is not recognised. But the use of the same knowledge by tinkering in western labs is accorded recognition by adapting the definition ways that are based towards western science and western practitioners.

4. The TNC Bias in TRIPs

With the Uruguay Round of GATT, the industrial patent and IPR regimes have been expanded geographically and in terms of subject matter. Western style IPR regimes have been universalised through the TRIPs agreement.

The TRIPs Agreement of GATT is not a product of negotiations. It has been imposed by transactional corporations on the citizens of the world, by manipulating the government of industrialised countries. The framework for the TRIPs agreement was conceived and shaped by the Intellectual Property Committee (USA), Keidanren (Japan), UNICE (Europe). IPC is a coalition of thirteen major US Corporations dedicated to the finalisation of TRIPs in GATT. The members of IPC are Bristol Myers, Dupont, General Electric, General Motors, Hewlett Packard, IBM, Johnson and Johnson, Merck, Monsanto, Pfizer, Rockwell and Warner. Keidanren is the Japanese Federation of Economic Organisations. UNICE is the Union of Industrial and Employees Confederations of Europe and is recognised as an official spoksman for European Business and Industry.

These groups worked closely to introduce intellectual property protection into GATT. James Enyart of Monsanto, commenting on the IPC strategy states :

> Besides selling the concepts at the home the document was presented to the staff of the GATT Secretariat. We also took the opportunity to present it to the Geneva based representatives of a large number of countries. What I have described to you is absolutely unprecedented GATT. Industry has identified a major problem in international trade. I crafted a solution, reduced it to a

concrete proposal and solid it to our own and other governments. Industries and traders of world commerce have played simultaneously the role of patients, the diagnosticians and the prescribing physicians.

It is this usurpation of all the rights of diverse social groups by commercial interests that has led to the displacement of ethical, ecological and social concern from the substance of the TRIPs agreement. TRIPs is not the result of democratic negotiations between the larger public and the commercial interests or between industrialised countries and the Third World. It is the imposition of values and interests of northern TNCs on the diverse societies and cultures of the world.

At the conceptual level, Trade-Related intellectual Property Rights (TRIPs) are restrictive, being by definition weighted in favour of transnational corporations, and against citizens in general, and particularly Third World peasants and forest-dwellers. People every where innovate and create. In fact, the poorest have to be the most innovative, since they have to create their means of survival while it is daily threatened. Women have been important innovators and protectors of seeds and genetic resources. Limitations to the ownership of intellectual property rights, as construed in the trade negotiations, operate on a number of levels.

The first is the shift from common to private rights : the preamble of the TRIPs agreement states that intellectual property rights are recognized only as private rights. This excludes all kinds of knowledge, ideas, and innovations that take place in the 'intellectual commons,' in villages among farmers, in forests among tribals and even in universities among scientists. TRIPs is therefore a mechanism to privatize the intellectual commons and de-intellectualize civil society, so that in effect, the mind becomes a corporate monopoly.

The second limitation is that intellectual property rights are recognized only when knowledge and innovation generate profits, not when they meet social needs. According to Article 27(1), to be recognized as an IPR, innovation must be capable of industrial application. Only profits and capital accumulation are recognized as viable uses of creativity. Under corporate control the social creativity and social good are discounted.

The most significant limitation of IPRs is achieved by way of the prefix 'trade-related'. Most innovation by women peasants and tribals is for domestic, local and public use, not for international trade; TNCs innovate for the sole purpose of increasing their share in global markets and international trade; and TRIPs in GATT will only enforce TNCs rights to monopolize all production, distribution and profits at the cost of all citizens and small producers.

Article 27 on patentable matter is a clear indication that all prior boundary conditions on patent regimes have been removed. Article 27(1) states that patents shall be available for any inventions, whether products or processes, in all fields of technology, provided that they are new, involve an inventive step, and are capable of industrial application.

This nullifies the exclusions built into national patent laws for the protection of the public and the national interest. For example, in the Patent Act of India, 1970, methods of agriculture and horticulture were excluded, were not patentable, whereas the TRIPs text includes these as patentable. Under the Indian Patent Act, only process patents can be granted to food, medicines, drugs and chemical products, but under the WTO, the Third World will have to grant product patents also in this area.

Even though a transition period of 10 years has been given to introduce a product patent regime for agrichemical and pharmaceuticals, Article 70(8) and 70(9) of the TRIPs agreement require that present patent applications be received and exclusive marketing right (EMR) granted against them beginning with 1st January 1995, the date of coming into being of the World Trade Organisation.

Article 70(9) also makes EMRs dependent on the claimant having obtained a patent and marketing approval for claim in another country. Since it is TNCs that operate in more than one country, these clauses for the implementation of TRIPs are clearly biased in their favour and against Indian nationals especially the rural communities, who have neither the resources nor the means to apply for patents outside India.

5. The Inadequacy of Western Patent Regimes for Protection of Biodiversity and Indigenous Knowledge

As stated above, existing patent regimes are biased in favour of large TNCs with interests cutting across pharmaceuticals and agrichemicals. Thus, the top fourteen countries dominate plant patents.

These patent systems are in any case inappropriate to the subject matter of biodiversity or living resources. They were not designed for this domain. As stated by John Hoxic in *A Patent Attorney's View*,

Top 14 Owners of Biotech Plant Patents

Company	*Country*	*No. of Patents*
Monsanto	USA	18
DNA Plant Technology	USA	17
Pioneer Hi-Bred	USA	11
Mycogen	USA	10
ICI/Zeneca	UK	7
Ciba/Geigy	Switzerland	6
Du Pont	USA	6
Rockefeller Univ.	USA	5
Agracetus	USA	5
Agricultural Genetics	USA	4
Amoco	USA	4
Michigan State Univ.	USA	4
Lubrizol	USA	4

Source : RAFI Communique, July/Aug. 1995.

The patent system as we have it today was really very little changed by the Patent Act of 1952; it goes back to a period when invention was largely mechanical, followed by an electrical era. In both, invention was chiefly of physical objects. The language and much of the judicial treatment of the statutes is geared to that sort of invention. When chemical invention became more frequent…a problem arose of fitting chemical invention into a mold of words and a habit of thinking that were not developed with it in mind.

The shift from the chemical era to the age of biology creates new problems of patentability. Firstly, patents on biodiversity or products of biodiversity, or uses of biodiversity falsely claim properties of plant derived drugs as 'products of the mind' when they are actually products of plant biodiversity. Unlike mechanical and electrical artifacts, plant-based medicines are not merely a result of inventive human genius. They are based on existing properties and characteristic of diverse plants. The boundary between the 'product of nature' and the 'product of the mind' is therefore fizzy and blurred in the case of medicines from plants. Secondly, the use of medicinal plants in indigenous systems of knowledge is the basis of most patent claims by western enterprise. Indigenous systems are used and exploited, but not recognised or protected. Instead of recognition and protection being given to the innovation of traditional systems are based. Recognition and protection under western style patent regimes is given to minor modifications and tiny tinkering of indigenous knowledge systems by practitioners of western sciences. Patents cannot offer protection to the intellectual heritage of practitioners of indigenous medical traditions. The knowledge of utilisation of biodiversity for particular health problems which is available in traditional systems is not patentable by indigenous practitioners since the criteria of potentiality are : (a) novelty, (b) non-obviousness, (c) industrial application.

Within the indigenous tradition undertaken by traditional practitioners, the knowledge is an ancient heritage, and hence is not 'novel' even though it is based on innovation. Being traditional is by definition not new. It, therefore, cannot satisfy criterion (a). Further, since indigenous medical systems are non-industrial but part of folk traditions or small-scale production processing and use, they also do not meet criterion (c).

However, when knowledge from these ancient systems is transferred to the west, translated into western systems for commercialisation on large-scale it gets treated as 'non-obvious' and having industrial application. There is thus a derecognition of the innovation embodied in indigenous systems and the possibility of claiming its appropriation as the innovative step. The knowledge that the Neem can be used for biopesticide or that *Phyllanthus niruri* can be used for jaundice cure is clearly part of indigenous knowledge and indigenous practice in India.

The principle that plant P is useful for U is therefore existing knowledge, and cannot be treated as novel. Further, given this principle, small variations in processing P for U are an obvious step. How then does such knowledge get patented and qualify is 'novel' and 'non-obvious'.

Translation or Creation

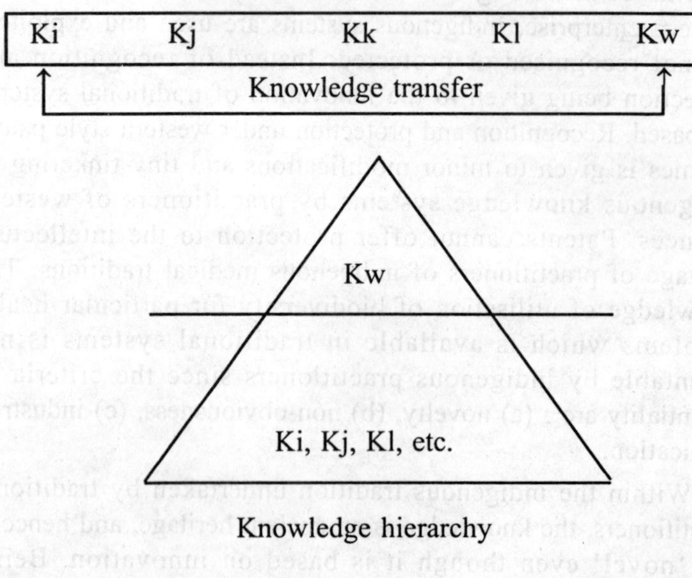

Knowledge hierarchy

Fig. 2.

The false claim to novelty is based on the existence of diverse and pluralistic knowledge systems. It is based on the fact that while such knowledge might exist in knowledge system Ki but it does not exist in the western knowledge system. The lateral transfer of knowledge with no epistemic value added, *i.e.*, mere translation of the knowledge that plant P is useful for purpose of U from system K to system Kw is taken as an innovation. Translation of Ki — Kw in a hierarchical perspective suggests a 'higher' level of knowledge content. Translation is misconstrued as the 'creation' of knowledge.

A sociological shift is thus fallaciously treaded as an epistemological shift. This fallacy of sociological and cultural displacement as an epistemological shift generating new knowledge is made possible because knowledge pluralities have been transformed into knowledge hierarchies as a result of colonial biases which have treated western knowledge as exclusively scientific and non-western knowledge systems as unscientific.

However, the difference in epistemological foundations does not make indigenous knowledge systems inferior, it just makes them different.

This diversity of knowledge need to be recognised and respected, and a pluralistic IPR regime needs to be evolved which makes it possible to recognise and respect indigenous knowledge, and protect the indigenous knowledge systems and practices and livelihoods based on it.

The criteria on which Lw is based fails to recognise Ki where is not w — *i.e* non-western knowledge systems. It is only when an element of Ki (i is not w) is transferred to Kw, that it is recognised, and it is then treated as an innovation in Kw. As a corollary, the interests and rights of Ci (i is not w) find no place in Lw, and are transferred to Cw, the scientific practitioners of western knowledge system w, in particular those backed by corporate capital.

It is the inappropriateness of existing IPR regimes like

patents for the protection of traditional knowledge systems and biodiversity, and the absence of a legal framework that protects the integrity of indigenous knowledge systems that leads to IPRs in their present restrictive forms becoming mechanisms for piracy.

The protection of indigenous knowledge systems as systems of innovation and the prevention of piracy requires a widening of legal regimes beyond the existing IPR regimes such as patents. In this context, it becomes clear that what are referred to as 'strong IPR regimes' for the perspective of economically powerful corporations of western countries are actually weak regimes from the perspective of people of countries like India with a rich biodiversity heritage and an ancient intellectual heritage of indigenous knowledge systems. What we need to evolve is a strong legal framework for biodiversity protection and the protection of our intellectual heritage. 'Strong' and 'weak' are therefore not absolute qualifications for IPR regimes but are relative to the social and economic objectives.

6. The Need for an Alternative to Western Style IPR Regimes

In an ecologically diverse and technologically plural society such as ours the objective of legal systems cannot be to merely protect the interest of transnational corporations or practitioners western science and technology systems. It has to be wide enough in scope to protect diverse economic organisations and diverse knowledge systems.

Indigenous knowledge systems aimed at self-provisioning and local self-reliance in nutrition and health care need criteria for protection different from the novelty and industrial application criteria for patents. Instead of individual right, such protection needs to be based on community rights and collective innovation. Instead of novelty criteria it needs to be based on heritage criteria and on innovation over time.

Indigenous knowledge producers innovate collectively. This innovation also takes place over time — it accretional, informal and over time. The knowledge evolves as it modifies, adapts and builds upon the existing knowledge. A redefinition of 'innovation' is therefore needed that reflects this process of innovation cumulatively over time, and collectively across a community. The current definition is based on a false and artificial construction of individual innovation as a one-shot in time. Neither in traditional indigenous systems, nor in western scientific tradition is innovation an isolated activity in the temporal or the social context.

Accordingly, a team of scientists and lawyers of the Third World Network have proposed to define 'innovation' as follows to reflect the innovation in indigenous systems in order to protect the 'collective rights' of indigenous innovators.

Innovation includes any collective and cumulative knowledge or technology of the use, properties, values and processes of any biological material or part thereof, rendered of any, or enhanced, use or value as a result of the said cumulative knowledge or technology whether documented, recorded, oral, written or howsoever otherwise existing including any alteration, modification, improvement thereof; and shall also include derivatives which utilize the knowledge of indigenous peoples and local communities in the commercialization of any product as well as to a more sophisticated process for extracting, isolating, or synthesizing the active chemical in the biological extracts or compositions used by the indigenous peoples.

Further, such a community rights (CR) regime needs to be the basis against which patent applications are considered. If indigenous innovations are protected by CRs, such innovations cannot be treated as novel — they have to be recognised as derived in obvious ways from prior innovations, with its associated set of rights. CRs thus set the boundary conditions, for IPRs in the era of TRIPs and the World Trade Organisations. (See Fig. 2)

Further, since the issue of piracy and IPR claims on indigenous knowledge has become a global pandemic and PRs have been globalised through GATT, steps need to be taken to ensure that CRs are the basis on which IPRs in any country are issued and that piracy of CRs can be challenged anywhere.

The inadequacy of existing IPR arrangements for the protection of indigenous knowledge and Indian medical systems makes the evolution of a *sui generis* system of community rights for traditional practitioners an urgent imperative. Any new IPR policy in India needs to be based on the recognition that the largest number of 'knowledge providers' in the area of biodiversity are practitioners of systems based on indigenous knowledge.

Knowledge is not 'created' when it is merely transferred to a lab practising western science in India, or to practitioners in the west. Protection of such transfer by IPRs is based on a false definition of 'innovation' and 'creation' — and it perpetuates piracy, both withing the country and internationally.

Piracy will eventually destroy our intellectual heritage by displacing our knowledge systems, our practices and our decentralised, self-reliant bodiversity-based economics. To stop this destruction, the granting of patents must not be made conditional to a screening of prior innovation and prior rights in the indigenous systems.

TRIPs has universalised the framework for IPR regimes on the assumption that the only knowledge is in western scientific journals. However, in the area of medicinal plants, patent claims are increasingly being based on indigenous knowledge that exists outside the information and communication systems of western scientific research in the language, epistemology and communications systems of diverse cultures and knowledge systems. The lack of recognition of these systems, and the lack of legal regimes to ensure their protection leads to the phenomena of piracy.

The establishment of a community rights regime would ensure that the sovereign rights to biodiversity are made real and the benefits from the biological resources and our knowledge tradition first flow to us. This would not prevent either innovation or our sharing of benefits with other countries. It would in fact ensure that what is rewarded is real innovation, and not mere piracy. It would, also ensure that overtime TNCs monopolies, strengthened through patents, do not block the flow of knowledge of how plants can heal and cure us.

The conflicts and debates unleashed by the introduction of IPRs in biodiversity have forced us to reassess the value of our biological and intellectual heritage. To stop the piracy of this and hence its destruction, the IPR and Biodiversity legislation being evolved has to define and defend our sovereign rights to our social creativity and our national wealth, in the past, in the present and the future.

It is to be remembered that what is being pirated is not one invention of one individual or corporation but the collective creativity and inventiveness of millions of people over millennia, a creativity that has shaped one civilizational distinctiveness and steadfastness and that is necessary for meeting the needs of our people in the future. We need to recognise that knowledge of medicinal plants has been evolved and perfected in our civilisation over thousand of years of innovation.

The issue of protection of knowledge of medicinal plants is not a narrow legal issue, or technical issue. It is an issue of the continuity and survival of the knowledge values of an ancient civilisation as reflected in the ancient hymn from the Rig Veda.

7

Status of Plant Genetic Resources Conservation and Utilization in Asia-Pacific Region

Introduction

PLANT GENETIC resources are elementary to sustainable agriculture and food security. The world has been largely demarcated into the gene rich and the gene poor regions depending upon the available diversity for different crop plant species and their wild relatives. The Asia-Pacific region is largely gene rich yet it faces challenges of sustainability due to various pressures, such as of population growth, poverty, hunger, deprivation and degradation of natural resource base. It is well recognized that conservation and proper management of plant genetic resources would ensure future economic growth and development.

Over the past three decades, the agricultural production has doubled and the world trade has increased three fold. The per capita availability of food has also increased from 2,300 kilo calories per day to 2,700 kilo calories (FAO, 1995). However, an estimated 800 million people still go to bed hungry due to population pressure, *i.e.* an increase of over 2,400 million in the world's population. As many as 192 million children under the age of five suffer from chronic or acute protein and energy deficiencies. Current statistics for Asia-Pacific region are equally depressing. The region holds two-thirds of the world's poor and under-nourished people. One person in every five does not have access to two square meals a day. On the contrary, it is encouraging to note that the Global Assessment of Nutrition and Development made by WHO and FAO in 1992 indicated that Asia and the Pacific, among all the regions of the world, showed substantial improvement in reduction of both poverty and hunger. Nevertheless, it is of concern that the largest number of impoverished hungry people are still found in this region, and that such a situation needs to be addressed with appropriate strategies.

Agriculture is the most predominant occupation in the Asia-Pacific Region. The peasants' backyards and home gardens predominate with traditional agriculture. Preponderance of a wide diversity in species/varieties/forms/local landraces has ensured susceptibility and less vulnerability to losses in cases of severe calamities due to the evolutionary co-existence with endemic diseases and pests. The variety of plants, including semi-domesticated forms, grown from seeds or vegetative propagules over generations, have been selected for the desired attributes, consciously or sub-consciously, and have inherited plasticity and adaptability in diverse niches/ecological habitats. Such agricultural ecosystems, predominantly covered under traditional farming systems, have fostered genetic diversity in favour of harmony, co-existence and sustainability.

The rural farming communities and the indigenous people have continued to maintain agro-biodiversity over the millennium. At the same time, they applied selection and improved materials to suit their needs and preferences or to counter environmental stresses. This continuum has been essential to their livelihood and survival. There has been no clear-cut distinction for them between conservation and development and, hence, their intervention in the past accelerated the process of evolution of agro-biodiversity. In general, the magnitude of this effect is more manifest in the gene rich regions in contrast with their counterparts, who would obviously need more diverse, alien resource base rich regions in contrast with their counterparts, to sustain and enhance their agricultural productivity and production in future. Nevertheless, there is a global need to maintain the agro-biodiversity with ample understanding of intrinsic values, input and technology. This is clearly highlighted in the global plan of action and must go hand in hand. The gene rich regions have to come forward to address the issues of conservation for sustainable use, with the required thrust and also assured support/resources.

Asia, as a whole, covers one-fifth of the total area under agriculture in the world. The Asia and the Pacific region is a highly populated region possessing above 3.1 billion people, being 57 per cent of the total world population, as compared to 12 and 9 per cent represented by African and Latin American continents, respectively. Surprisingly, this enormous population is inhabiting just one-fifth of the total land area and 57 per cent of this entire population lives in Asia-Pacific Region alone. Further, nearly three-fourth (72.3 per cent) of the global population engaged in agriculture comes from this region. The Asia-Pacific Region represents 20.9 per cent of the world's cultivated area including permanent area under crops. It has recorded nearly two-fifth world production of food crop commodities including cereals, roots and tuber crops, pulses, oilseeds, vegetables and fruits. The proportion of cereal crop production has been very impressive (48 per cent) and, in terms of rice alone, this region produced over 91 per cent as total global rice production. The share of agriculture in Gross Domestic Production (GDP) was recorded to be 26.7 per cent in 1994 (APAARI, 1997). Some of the countries in the region showing a high percentage were Laos (57.4 per cent), and those on the lower side were Republic of Korea (7.2 per cent), Thailand (11.1 per cent), Cook Islands (12.5 per cent), Malaysia (14.8 per cent) and Indonesia (16.6 per cent).

The Asia-Pacific region is by and large poverty stricken. A considerably higher percentage of poverty has been recorded in Vietnam (54 per cent), the Philippines (45 per cent), Bangladesh (44 per cent) and Myanmar (35 per cent), in comparison with a mean value of 30 per cent for the developing countries.

The affluence of human resource in the Asia-Pacific region as a whole is well supplemented with abundant natural resources and rich biodiversity. Asia contributes about 90 per cent of the total global rice production estimated at 518.5 million metric tonnes in 1990. Interestingly, of the total rice production, more than 90 per cent is met from the *indica* types produced mainly in tropical countries, whereas the rest, less than to 10 per cent, comprises of *japonica* types produced mostly in Japan, Korea and high elevation areas of other countries in the region. Some countries of the Asia-Pacific region are already self-sufficient in rice. Indonesia, having achieved self-sufficiency for rice in 1994, has placed an utmost priority to sustain the same. Vietnam too is self-sufficient and even manages to export about 2 million tonnes of rice annually. Myanmar has placed high priority for targeted production and enhancing its acreage to 5 million ha. South Asia, with an annual production of 157 million tonnes accounted for 23 per cent of world's production and nearly one-third of the production of the Asia-Pacific region alone. India and Bangladesh contribute significantly to the rice production, being 75 and 18 per cent, respectively.

Production systems in the Pacific Island countries are different from the rest of the Asia-Pacific region. Mostly root crops featured under this system, although some other commodities such as squash in Tonga and rice, ginger and vegetables in Fiji are considered important components of their respective agricultural systems. Papua New Guinea, Western Samoa and Solomon Islands have sweet potato and taros as dominant component of agriculture. Tapioca also provides major source of dietary carbohydrate (starch) to several countries in South Asia, South-East Asia and the Pacific. Agricultural transformation has already set in, although slowly, having severe impact on existing agricultural crops and farming practices, in the Pacific Island countries.

The Asia-Pacific region has been categorized into four sub-regions, namely, the South Asia, the South-East Asia, the East Asia and the Pacific Island countries, for the purpose of setting out common research and development priorities. A brief introductory account of each sub-region is as follows :

South Asia

The South Asia sub-region includes Bangladesh, Bhutan, India, Maldives, Nepal, Pakistan and Sri Lanka. It constitutes one of the cradles of world agriculture and houses the larger part of the Vavilovian "Hindustani Centre of Origin". The sub-region is endowed with rich genetic diversity in plant genetic resources besides a wide variation in climate, soil and agro-ecology.

The sub-region represents 21 per cent of global population, which resides on 3 per cent of the land area and includes more than 50 per cent of the world's malnourished children (APAARI, 1996). During the past over three decades (*i.e.* from 1960 onwards), the agricultural production in the sub-region has registered a tremendous increase. In several commodities, the growth has been recorded up to 300 per cent. The impact of green revolution has been very impressive. However, at the same time, productivity growth rates have been on a decline; the availability of pulse reduced from 30-40g/day to 15-16g/day. This, together, could be attributed to several factors, including (i) the ramified areas or the dryland agriculture did not record as much production increase as the other areas, (ii) the research and development approaches were commodity-based rather than system-based, and (iii) the population pressure has been negating production increases. The decline in growth of production due to a decrease in productivity has passed a serious concern and the other disturbing trends include increased uniformity (homogeneity) in crop stands, the impoverishment of already resource-poor farmers and, above all, serious loss of genetic diversity.

In the recent years, the green revolution has had a tremendous, positive impact on cereal production thereby providing ample food security. It also altered the prevalent agricultural environment, particularly the sustainable agro-ecosystems, to a certain extent, being largely attributed to preferential acceptability of high yielding varieties/cultivators albeit with narrow genetic base and requiring high imputs, to attain higher production gains. The increased use of chemicals, such as fertilizers, pesticides and herbicides had an alarming effect on the agro-biodiversity, particularly the co-existing species and the microbes. Further, the second generation problems, which need to be addressed specifically in order to achieve sustainable growth, include water logging, salinization, soil erosion, surface and ground water decline and contamination. The foremost concern is, however, that the modern transformation of agriculture is also resulting in the irreversible loss of landrace diversity in crop plant species, their wild relatives and in the habitats. The attention has also to be focused to avert poverty, particularly in the stressed and diverse areas of rainfed agriculture system which occupy a major portion of the sub-region.

India, a large country in the sub-region, occupies approximately 90 per cent area and 85 per cent population (960 million people) of the entire Asia-Pacific. Each of the other countries less than even 4 per cent of the total area. Maldives, the smallest country situated in the Indian Ocean and occupying merely 0.10 per cent area, is represented by 1190 coral islands. Bangladesh is the most densely populated country in the sub-region (8.36 persons/sq. km), representing about 11 per cent of the total population of the sub-region. Its population density is very high compared to India (285 persons/sq.km). Pakistan, Nepal and Sri Lanka represent 13, 2 and 2 per cent population, respectively, whereas Bhutan has less than 0.2 per cent population of the sub-region. In terms of population growth, Maldives recorded the highest growth and population density in the sub-region whereas Bhutan recorded the lowest.

The climate varies from tropical/subtropical in southern region to temperate/alpine in the Himalayan region. The trans-Himalayan region, adjoining the Tibet plateau and China represents cold arid desert. The Maldives islands are flat with elevations rising high upto 2.5 metres. Sri Lanka possesses low mountain ranges insides the island country. Bhutan, India, Nepal and Pakistan have Himalayan and Hindukush mountain ranges, the upland alluvial fertile Indus valley and Indo-Gangetic plains encompassing large agricultural land. Hot *Thar* desert in western parts of India and eastern part of Pakistan and the cold desert in the trans-Himalayan region provide specific climatic niches. Nepal also has the fertile *Tarai* area in the foothills adjoining the Indian Gangetic plains. Bhutan is land locked in mostly mountainous region with rich fertile valleys and natural forest cover dominating major part of the country.

The sub-region of South Asia is subjected to several natural hazards like earthquakes (Hindukush and Himalayan region), droughts, cyclones, tornadoes, severe thunderstorms and floods. Bangladesh and the adjoining parts of northeast and eastern India are flooded during the summer monsoon season. This natural phenomenon generally renders large proportion of its population constrained with no other option that to live on and cultivate the flood prone land. In the Himalayan region (Bhutan, India, Nepal and Pakistan), landslides during the rainy season are frequent in the fragile Himalayan mountains. This *inter alia* results in considerable loss of biodiversity, particularly the wild relatives of crop plant species and the medicinal plant wealth. The climate change, particularly resulting in the sea rise, often threatens the low lying islands on Maldives and coastal region of Bangladesh and adjoining India falling in the Bay of Bengal. Predominant environmental issues being faced by the South Asia sub-region are : (i) over population; (ii) deforestation; (iii) over grazing/over exploitation of natural vegetation; (iv) soil erosion; (v) loss of biodiversity and (vi) pollution. Recent years have witnessed a rapid loss of generic diversity that was hitherto preponderant in the agricultural systems of the sub-region.

The Agriculture and the Natural Forest Ecosystem

Agriculture is the predominant occupation of the people of the South Asia, having a prominence in the sub-region's economy. It has an ancient history, being practised over the past thousands of years. The process led to the domestication of several plant species and has given rise to the enormous amount of diversity of forms in agri-horti and silvi-forestry plant species.

Over 90 per cent of human resource in Bhutan and Nepal and 45 per cent to 65 per cent in the other countries of the sub-region is engaged in agriculture. Agriculture accounts for about 30 per cent of GDP in India, over 50 per cent in Nepal and Bhutan and 25 to 35 per cent in other countries of the sub-region. Until the turn of the century, agriculture appears to have remained predominantly of maintaining such kind of farming systems. Commercial agriculture in the sub-region has been practised to a little extent. However, some new trends towards commercialization of agriculture and agricultural products are emerging due to the opening of seed industry and globalization efforts.

In recent years, the contribution of agriculture to gross domestic product (GDP) has been observed to decline. It has become increasingly difficult to maintain economic development by the countries of the South Asia sub-region solely through the agricultural production. Efforts to diversify these economies by exploiting natural resources and cheap labour for production of industrial goods and other value added products have not yielded desired results although trends appear to be encouraging. An inadequate infrastructure and low level of technologies could be among the important underlying factors. Agriculture is sure to continue playing an important role in future economic development and growth and would constitute a primary factor in the world trade.

The principal agricultural crops of the South Asia sub-region are rice, wheat, maize, coarse grains, sugarcane, jute, grain lagumes (Pulses), oilseed, potato, sweet potato, other tuber crops, fruits and vegetables and cashew. India, being quite advanced agriculturally, has emerged as world's largest producer and exporter of tea, second largest producer of rice, sorghum, groundnut and sugarcane, fruits and vegetables, third largest producer of wheat, cotton, rapeseed and mustard and seventh largest producer of potatoes. Pakistan and Bangladesh have attained considerable success in terms of production and export of cotton and jute, respectively, and Sri Lanka in coffee. Countries of this sub-region at large have strived hard and achieved a high degree of self-sufficiency in food production yet many are still net importers of food, fibre, pulses and oilseeds in substantial quantities. In several areas of the sub-region, food scarcity and undernourishment are still common. According to UNICEF the percentage of under-nourished children in the age group of 5 years is 67 per cent in Bangladesh, 53 per cent in India, 49 per cent in Nepal and 38 per cent in Sri Lanka. Maldives meets nearly 95 per cent of the country's demand for food through imports, although there is sufficient land available for agricultural production. Rice is the predominant crop followed by wheat. The decline in agriculture in the recent years is also due to a high cost of production as compared with the processed, imported foodstuff.

It is estimated that 53 per cent of the total land area of the sub-region is classifiable as arable land and 24 per cent as forest and woodland. The ratio of arable to forest land ranges from 5:1 each in Bangladesh and Pakistan, 2:1 in India, 3:1 in Maldives, 1:3 in Bhutan and 1:2 each in Nepal and Sri Lanka. Timber and other wood products are scarce due to low production and low supply in view of the increasing demands.

Over half of the land with agricultural potential in the sub-region is semi-arid; most of it exists in India. This includes 38 per cent moist semi-arid (productive rainfed land with attainable yields greater than 40 per cent) and 13 per cent dry semi-arid (productive and marginally productive). 22 per cent of the agricultural land of the sub-region, including about half of Nepal and Sri Lanka and a quarter of India, is sub-humid (productive rainfed land, with attainable yields greater than 40 per cent of potential constraint free yields).. About 40 per cent of the agricultural land in Bhutan is humid and 50 per cent is marginal (marginally productive rainfed land, with attainable yields of 20-40 per cent of potential constraint-free yields). This kind of marginal land also occurs in Nepal (30 per cent) and Sri Lanka

(17 per cent). About 73 per cent of agricultural land in Bangladesh, 18 per cent in Nepal, 14 per cent in Sri Lanka and 6 per cent in India is naturally flooded land (productive low land flooded or waterlogged for greater part of the year with attainable yields greater than 40 per cent of potential constraint free yields). The latter constitutes about 10 per cent of the total agricultural land in the sub-region.

Pakistan, possessing 27.7 per cent agricultural land as a percentage of total land and agricultural population accounting for 51.1 per cent of the total population, is situated in proximity to major centres of diversity of many plant species. The ancient trade route from China to western Asia passes through the sub-region resulting in the introduction/migration of several economically useful plant species. Over the centuries, rich diversity has been built in many of the agricultural crops, fruits and nuts, particularly in remote valleys in the north; both human and natural selection have played a prominent role in this process. The excavations at the ancient sites of Mohenjodaro and Harappa have revealed existence of early agriculture in the sub-region, particularly the Indian sub-continent. Several crops, including wheat, barley, rice, cotton and sesame were discovered to have been under cultivation in the ancient times.

South-East Asia

The South-East Asia sub-region includes the area lying mainly in and around the Malayan peninsula, sharing similar floristic wealth for agriculture and forestry, its composition and distribution. The countries that fall in the sub-region included Brunei, Cambodia, Indonesia, Laos, Malaysia, Myanmar, the Philippines, Singapore, Thailand and Vietnam. The region possesses 300 to 400 million ethnically and culturally diverse people. A majority of the poor in the sub-region are located in few countries, namely, Cambodia, Laos, Vietnam and Myanmar. The population below poverty line in Vietnam, the Philippines, Myanmar and Thailand is reported to be 54, 45, 35 and 30 per cent, respectively.

Agriculture is an important sector in the sub-region to meet the growth in food demand and economy. It accounts for 34-57 per cent share in the Gross Domestic Product (GDP) in different countries of the sub-region. The share of labour force in agriculture has remained consistent at approximately 70 per cent. The principal farming system is rice based which constitutes the staple food. The other crops grown as a part of the complex farming systems vary from country to country, as given below :

Cambodia	: Maize, rubber, groundnut, soyabean, sesame, rice, jute, cotton, tobacco.
Indonesia	: Coffee, rubber, tea, coconut, rice, sugarcane and tropical fruits.
Malaysia	: Rubber, oil palm, coconut, cocoa, rice, grain legumes, vegetable crops and tropical fruits.
Philippines	: Rice, maize, fruits crops, coconut and sugarcane.
Thailand	: Fruit crops, field crops, plantation crops.
Vietnam	: Rice, maize, sweet potato, yams, coconut, sugarcane, coffee and cacao.

Agriculture has traditionally been the most dominant sector in the economy of South-East Asia until very recently. About 90 per cent of the population still thrive on agriculture in Cambodia. The plantation and industrial crops have, however, received greater attention in some countries, namely, Malaysia and Indonesia, due to their export potential. In Malaysia, the contribution of agriculture to the National Gross Domestic Production (GDP) has also declined from 29 per cent in 1970 to 14 per cent in 1994, primarily due to industrialization. The agriculture is dominated by plantation crops like oil palm, rubber and cacao; among food crops, rice is the most predominant and this is followed by fruits and vegetables.

In the Philippines, 24 per cent and 20 per cent of the population derives livelihood from two main crops, namely, rice and maize, respectively. In addition, substantial area falls under coconut, sugarcane, Manila hemp, banana, pineapple and mango.

Agricultural exports from the Philippines contribute 16.1 per cent of the total value of export. In Thailand's agriculture, primarily fruit crops, ornamentals and evergreen plants, account for 70 to 80 per cent of the economy of the country. Major fruit crops under cultivation include, banana, mango, mangosteen, durian, rambutan and pineapple. Plantation crops include rubber and oil palm. Rich industry mangosteen, durian, rambutan and pineapple. Plantation crops include rubber and oil palm. Rich industry also exists in ornamentals, orchids and other evergreen plants. Over 40 per cent GDP of Vietnam is accounted for by agricultural sector. The major crops include rice, maize, sweet potato, and cassava. Industrial crops like coffee, rubber, tea, groundnut and cashew, contribute to export earnings whereas vegetables and banana are generally grown for its own domestic consumption.

The Cambodian national economy is also largely agriculture based, mostly rainfed, mono-cropped and mainly under rice based farming system. Farmers are poor and they live under extreme agro-ecological and socio-economical constraints. Agricultural produce such as maize, soyabean, groundnut, sesame, jute, cotton and tobacco and other products such as fish and timber are less used by local people due to lack of technology and facilities for processing to improve the quality of product for food and other domestic consumption. The forest cover of Cambodia is diverse. Different types include mangrove, flood forest, bamboo forest, coniferous forest, dry deciduous and moist deciduous rainforest or moist evergreen forest, moist mountain forest and evergreen forest. These forest ecosystems occur at varying altitudes or climatic conditions. However, over 95 per cent area of the country is situated below elevation of 1000 metres above average sea level. Rice constitutes the predominant crop followed by maize. Among legumes, soyabean is important followed by mungbean. The oilseed crops include groundnut and sesame. Further, among commercial crops, sugarcane followed by jute and tobacco are commonly grown. Vegetables occupy very large area under cultivation; sweet potato is more common whereas cassava is also sparsely cultivated.

Indonesia is an archipelagic country, lying between longitude 95°E and 141°E and latitude 6°N and 11°S, between the two continents of Asia and Australia. It constitutes the largest archipelago in the world, comprising of at least 17,000 islands situated in the Indian and the Pacific oceans. Its total land area comprises 191 million hectares (5,100 km in length) with 317 million hectares being under exclusive economic zone of its territorial waters. Indonesia has also the longest coastline in the world, which is approximately 81,100 km long. The 5 major islands comprise Sumatra (47.5 million ha), Java (13.25 million ha), Kalimantan, Southern part of Borneo (53.5 million ha), Sulawesi (18.6 million ha) and Irian Java (41.5 million ha). In addition, there are two major islands of smaller size, namely, Nusa Tenggara (8 million ha) and Malukai (the Moluccas, 7.8 million ha). Each of these islands has its own peculiar physiographical as well as biological characteristics.

Myanmar, occupying an area of 315,810 sq. km. and extending climatically from the subtropics to the tropics, lies between 0.58'N and 93°10'E and 101°99'E longitudes. Its climate is dominated by the south-west monsoon and is greatly influenced by the height and direction of mountain ranges running north to south. Myanmar can be divided into four physiographic regions which form the basis for agriculture, (i) mountains and hills occupying the north, west and east of the country (hilly region), (ii) central area of rice plains and low hills and terraces, (iii) delta plains forming the alluvium of the Ayeyarwaddy silting river, and (iv) coastal strips comprising narrow alluvial plains and rising mountainous terrain. Myanmar possesses a population of about 46 million people, concentrated in villages. In general, the farm holdings are very small (0.2 to 16 ha). The main staple crop of Myanmar, like in other South-East Asian countries, is rice which occupies over 0.4 million ha each year, being 50 per cent of the total cultivated area. The other important crops include pulses, sesame, groundnut, cotton, jute, maize and wheat.

Thailand is situated in mainland of South-East Asia within the boundary of the Indo-Malayan peninsula. It is small-sized country, comprising areas covered by reserved forests, agricultural land, grassland and wasteland. Almost entire land is used for growing rice and other field crops, fruits and plantation crops. Rainfed agriculture comprises 84 per cent while irrigated area occupies nearly 16 per cent of the total cropped land. The vegetation is divided into two main zones; lower tropical rain forests (peninsula and hill slopes upto 600 m) and the upper tropical forests (beyond 600 in elevation). The upper storey of forest canopy is mainly occupied by gigantic tree species (*e.g. Depterocarpus, Hopea* and *Shorea* spp. etc.).

The Philippines covers a total land area of approximately 185,328 sq. km., which constitutes about 2 per cent of the total land area of the world. There are 7107 islands and islets clustered into three major groups Luzon, Visayas and Mindanao. Of these Luzon and Mindanao comprise almost two largest islands with land area of 10,500 and 9,500 sq. km. respectively. Geographically, the Philippines is about 1000 km. from the south-east coast of mainland Asia, lying on the western region of the Pacific Ocean. It lies between 21°20'N and 4°3'N latitudes and 116°53'E and 126°36'E longitudes, covering an area of about two million hectares. Major area is inhabited by the indigenous communities occupying forest ecotones which interestingly accounts for half (15 million ha) of the country's total land area. The Philippines has a tropical and maritime climate characterized by high temperature, high humidity and abundant rainfall, similar to many South-East Asian countries, namely, Indonesia and Malaysia. The country has two marked seasons, dry and wet. On the western shore facing the South China Sea, the dry season generally begins in December and ends in May with the wet season extends the rest of the year.

Vietnam covers an area of 230,000 sq. km. and has a population of 72 million people. The country stretches from latitude 8°30'N to 23°30'N providing a very diverse physiography and climatic conditions. North Vietnam is characterized by high rugged mountains in the north-west, north-east and north-south directions become very cold in winter. The west side of central Vietnam is dominated by the Truongson ranges from north to south making a natural border between Vietnam and Laos. From northern to south, Vietnam can be divided into 7 agro-ecological zones : (i) the north zone; mainly mountains and mid lands with temperate to subtropical climatic, (ii) the north-west zone mainly mountainous with predominantly subtropical conditions; (iii) the Red river delta including the Mekong river delta with vast plain zone, with dry fertile soil, subtropical climate and cold winter; (iv) north central zone, mainly of mountainous highlands with a narrow strip of non-fertile soil; (v) coastal central zone with typical tropical climate and fertile soil; (vi) Central plateau with fertile tropical climate and fertile soils, and (vii) Mekong river delta which comprises largest plain with fertile soils, plentiful water resources and typical tropical climate.

Vietnam's economy is agriculture based; cultivated areas cover over 5 million ha and crop production constitutes two-third of the entire agriculture products. Main staple food crops of Vietnam are rice, maize, sweet potato, cassava; industrial crops include coffee, rubber, tea, groundnut, coconut and cashew. Sugarcane, cotton and jute are used mainly for domestic consumption. Fruit crops occupy 29,000 ha and banana constitutes the main export crop. Important grain legumes include soyabean and mungbean. Both temperate and subtropical vegetable crops are grown in Vietnam. Production has increased rapidly in all the agricultural crops and Vietnam ranks third in terms of rice export, being 2 million tonnes annually. It is also an important exporter of coffee and rubber. Forests account for 19 million ha occupying 60 per cent of the national territory, which has drastically reduced to 28 per cent during the last few decades with an estimated loss of 600,000 ha.

Agriculture has traditionally been the dominant sector in the economy of the South-East Asian region although recent developments in the industrial and service sectors in Singapore and Malaysia have led to the decline in the share of agriculture in the economy of these countries. In Malaysia, the Philippines and Thailand, traditional cultivators of crop species have been replaced by improved varieties. This trend is most apparent in fruits; for example, in cases of rambutan in Malaysia and guava in the Philippines. There has also been a definite replacement of traditional cultivars of rice and maize with the modern varieties in many areas in Malaysia, the Philippines and Thailand.

The main forest types in the sub-region are the tropical rainforests. In Indonesia, Malaysia, the Philippines, Thailand and Vietnam, depending on the elevation the forests are further classified into lower tropical rain forests, from sea level to 600 m in Thailand or 1000 m in the Philippines above average sea level, and lower mountain forests, from 600-900 m in Thailand or above 1000 m in the Philippines. At the higher elevations in Indonesia, a different forest type (the sub-alpine) is also found.

East Asia

This sub-region includes the countries of People's Republic of China, the Democratic People's Republic of Korea (DPR Korea), Japan, Mongolia and the Republic of Korea. The climate ranges from upland temperate to sub-tropical with varying population densities and land use pattern. China is large country in Asia, its area is more than 80 per cent of the East Asia sub-region. Republic of Korea has the highest population density in the sub-region followed by Japan, DPR Korea and China. Mongolia has one of the highest population growth rates in Asia, but its population density is very low. In China, Japan and the Republic of Korea, population pressure has resulted in a low ratio of forest area per capita. Japan is the second most powerful economy in the world, but the contribution of agriculture to its GDP and the proportion of labour force engaged in agriculture is very low. In contrast, agriculture is the main occupation in China whereas nearly 80 per cent of Mongolia's agricultural land is used for grazing purposes.

The sub-region includes the most populous country *i.e.* China and also other developed/advanced developing countries, such as,

Japan, China and Korea. It is several mega cities of the world located here. The population density in the sub-region is three times higher than that of the world. A traditional dependence of relatively higher population on agriculture is evident in China whereas Japan is highly industrialized. Above that, the cultural realization of the importance of agriculture for the economic development and farmer's prosperity in the sub-region has a long history. However, with the development of national economies, majority of the population depending on agriculture in sub-region, particularly China, moved to and concentrated in the urban, industrial centres. Whereas the total population of China, Japan and Korea expanded rapidly in the last 20 years, the farm population has declined sharply in Japan and Korea, particularly since the 70s, mainly due to industrialization and urbanization. Contrary to this, the total farm population in China increased from 685.7 million during the period 1970-90. This is attributed partly to the expansion of total population and partly to the slow rate of farm depopulation in this country. However, China is also likely to face a sharp decline in the total farm population with the further development of its national industry. The proportion of farm population to total population has decreased in all these countries during 1970-90.

The agriculture accounted for a relatively large share in the total Gross Domestic Product (GDP) of China, being 21 per cent, a mere 7.2 per cent for the Republic of Korea and a negligible value for Japan. The percentage of population dependent on agriculture in China, as labour force, was high whereas, in contrast, Japan and Korea, both located in the same sub-region had a very small proportion of their population engaged in agriculture. The labour force employed in agriculture in 1990 accounted for 73.6, 14.0 and 15.3 per cent of the total population in China, Japan and Korea, respectively.

In the past, agriculture in East Asian countries was characterized by small scale farming with low crop productivity. The land holdings in China, Japan and Korea, have been only about 0.5 to 1.4 ha as against average farm household areas in

Australia and USA of 2,800 ha and 182 ha, respectively. The labour productivity agriculture in these three countries has been obviously lower than that in the western countries. The potential for further developing land area for agriculture is also extremely limited in Japan and Korea. Of the 2.1 million ha cultivated area in Korea, about 64 per cent (1.3 million ha) are covered under paddy for production of rice which comprises the principal staple food crop. In Japan, 54 per cent of total cultivated land is used as lowland whereas remaining 36 per cent cultivated area in Korea and 46 per cent in Japan are uplands.

In China, a relatively lower proportion of lowland to upland fields has been observed. About 27 per cent of the cultivated land is used for the production of rice crops. It may be stated that farming in the entire Asia sub-region is primarily agriculture based, particularly the rice production. In 1990, the global production of major crops reached 2,112 million tons, 43.6 per cent of which came from the Asian region. In rice alone, the Asian region, contributed 90 per cent of the total production in the world and the trend in the total production have been further increasing. In addition to rice, the sub-region grows sufficient quantity of maize, wheat, potato, some soyabean and barley. Of the two main groups of rice varieties grown in this region, namely, *indica* and *japanica* types are mainly produced in tropical areas, and account for over 90 per cent of total rice production. The production of *japanica* types is less than 10 per cent mainly being produced in Japan, Korea, and other high elevation areas. Under the open market system the *indica* types get good returns. However, the case is not the same with *japanica* types. This poses a serious problem in Japan and Korea because the price of rice in South-East Asia is lower than that of the international market. In the domestic market, however, it is higher by five to seven times than that of the international market.

Pacific Island Countries

The Pacific island countries include islands of Fiji, Papua New Guinea, the Cook island, Solomon islands, Western Samoa,

Vanuatu, Federal Polynesia, Kiribati, Wallis Fruit Island, Tokelau and Tuvalu. The two developed countries, namely, Australia and New Zealand fall adjacent, in the Oceania region.

The Pacific region includes countries and territories lying between 110°E and 120°W longitude and 30°N and 55°S latitude. The population of the sub-region is made up primarily of Melanesians, Polynesians with mixture of Malayas, Chinese, Japanese and Indians. Substantial diversity occurs in nearly half a million square kilometre of the area in the region, which is spread over 30 km^2 of ocean. The ecological typographies in the sub-region can be broadly categorized into three main groups, namely : (i) large volcanic islands, rich in biological and physical resources; (ii) intermediate size volcanic islands, having rich soil but no mineral wealth. The details of islands covered under each category are as follows :

The island of Papua New Guinea (PNG) is the second largest in the world. It lies between 3.5° and 12° south of the equator in the region of hot-wet tropics. The island is approximately 3,500 km. from east to west with an area of around 775,000 square km. Papua New Guinea also includes the large islands of Manus, New Britain, New Ireland, Buka and Bougainville and several islands off the eastern tip. It has an area of about 475,000 sq. km. and a population of around 4 million. The population density varies from about 100 persons per sq. km. in the highland to about 61 person per sq. km. in the swampy areas of Gulf and western Provinces. The centre of the main island consists of series of mountain ranges (upto 4000 m) with populous upland country. The climate in coastal and larger island is generally hot and humid (25.35°C). The valleys of highland region are usually hot during the day time but cold at night. The general vegetation varies with elevation and rainfall and it has remarkable similarities with those occurring in Indonesia, Malaysia and other Pacific Island countries. The tropical rain forest of central and north-western parts of mainland possess rich diversity of species in flora and fauna. The forests are classified into five main categories — the low altitude forest on plains, the low altitude forests on upland, the lower Montane forest, the dry seasonal forest and the estuarine forest communities.

Agriculture is the major occupation of the people and farming constitutes 95 per cent of the economically active population, employment to 25 per cent of the work force, 14 per cent in foreign exchange and 25 per cent of the Gross Domestic Product (GDP). Small land holding farmers are the most productive component of the agriculture sector accounting for 90 per cent of all agriculture produce, 75 per cent of coffee, 65 per cent of coca, 66 per cent of coconut, 35 per cent of oil palm and almost all other crops. Crops such as yams, taros and banana, which were introduced from other sub-regions a few centuries ago, have become important. Traditionally the subsistence farmers, multiply and distribute their own seeds and planting materials. Majority of the crops grown are vegetatively propagated and planting materials of crops such as banana (*Musa* spp.), taros, cassava (*Manihot esculentum* Crantz), albika (*Abelmoschus manihot* L. Medik) and several other vegetable crops are maintained in old gardens and backyards.

The farming system adopted and practised in the region is diverse and complicated. Indigenous people belong to different tribal communities and their ethnic groups have their bases in the villages. The land is owned by clans or families and an individual is given right as a member of that clan/family to use the land. Farmers live with a subsistence agricultural system and grow food crops, do hunting, collection of food from the forests and harvest of fish from waterways and marine products from the sea. The farming community lives very close to the nature and derives several of the basic needs from forests. The subsistence farmers grow diversity of good crops in their home gardens in the mixed cropping manner, usually at very high density. The succulent leafy vegetables are planted first, followed by root and fruit crops such as banana and other fruit trees. Sweet potato is the most predominant food crop in the highland areas whereas in the lowland, the cropping systems are generally very diverse, varying from one area to another.

The dry coastal areas of the central province follow a banana-yam-cassava based farming system. Yams (*Dioscorea* spp.) are usually harvested followed by banana and cassava. Taros (*Colocasia esculenta* L.) is more predominant in the wet lowland areas of Morobe province and in the atoll environment. Mostly diploid banana is widely cultivated in the Madang, New Britain, New Ireland, Morobe and the Sepik provinces. The triploid and tetraploid banana are more suitable to the drier areas of the Markham/Ramu valleys and the central province. Rich variability exists in banana. Yam (*Dioscorea* spp.) based cropping system are practised at some inland areas of east Sepik, Madang and the Trob and islands of the Milne Bay province. Sago (*Metroxylon* spp.) is predominant in low marshy land areas throughout the country and the crop is harvested from the natural stands. People inhabiting the areas of the Fly, Sepik, Ramu and the Puerari deltas closely follow the sago based cropping system often accompanied by root crops and leafy vegetables in marginal arable land as supplement to the sago.

The Solomon Islands consist of a double chain of about 990 islands, mainly of volcanic origin and extending from about 155°-170°E to 5°-12°S, well within the tropics. The country has a total land area of 28,000 km^2. It is bounded on the west by Papua New Guinea, on the south-west by Australia and by the islands, Ellice, Fiji and New Caledonia on the south and east. The 1986 census recorded the population at 285,000 with an annual growth rate of 3.5 per cent. Western Samoa is a small island nation in the Central South Pacific and it lies between latitude 13°S and 15°S very close to international dateline. Western Samoa possesses total land area of 2,830 sq. km. and the population is 165,000. The islands are of volcanic origin clearly visible in the form of several dormant volcanoes and lava fields. The kingdom of Tonga consists of three groups of small islands scattered over 290 sq. km. of South Pacific Ocean. 36 of the 150 islands of Tonga are inhabited. The total land area is 747 sq. km.

Unlike the other sub-regions, the principal for farming systems in the Pacific Island countries are based on sweet potato, taros, yams, cassava, coconut, oil palm, cacao, coffee and fruit trees. In the Solomon Islands, home gardens possess taros as the dominant species. It is more important since 90 per cent of the population depends on subsistence horticulture the Western Samoa's farming systems are characterized by closely interdependent production activities across the crops, livestock, fisheries and forestry species. Production of root crops such as gaint taros (*Alocacia macrorrhiza*), yams (*Dioscorea* spp.), *Zanthosoma* sp., taro (*Colocacia esculenta*) and cassava (Mannihot esculentum) predominates. However, taro, the main staple food, has been severely devastated by the taro leaf blight caused by *Phytophthora colocasiae*. In Tonga, the principal sector of the economy is agriculture and 70 per cent of the population depends on agriculture particularly root crops based farming system.

Importance of agriculture in the economy of the island countries varies to some extent. In the Cook Island, agriculture has been replaced by tourism. In Niue, the potential of agriculture is limited by the absence of surface water, scarcity of soil, small size of island and land tenure system. In recent years, however, some dramatic changes have occurred in the farming system and the cropping pattern. Squash has emerged as a lucrative cash crop in Tonga : A typical 3.3 ha farm would have 35-45 per cent of the area cropped and remaining one under fallow, at a given time of the year. About 60-80 per cent of land is occupied by yams, taros, cassava and sweet potato and the remaining area is cultivated under cash crops, namely, squash, vanilla, banana, pineapple and peanut, among others.

Landuse Pattern and Crop Production in Asia-Pacific Region

Selected indicators of food and agriculture development in Asia-Pacific region during the past ten years period (1985-1995) suggested that China, in the northeast Asia sub-region, possesses highest total land area while the arable land accounted only for 10 per cent. This was followed by Bangladesh and India, both in the South Asia sub-region, with 74 and 57 per cent of arable land and permanent cropped area, respectively. In the South-East Asia sub-region, Thailand (41 per cent) and among the Pacific Island countries, Tonga (67 per cent) and Western Samoa (43 per cent) indicated high percentage of land utilization. The region, as a whole, possessed highest percentage of arable and cropped land (16 per cent) as compared to rest of the world. Among the developed countries of the region, New Zealand and Japan have high percentage of arable and permanent crop land.

China ranked top in total land area (932.6 million ha) with highest population (122.14 million). It was followed by India (297.3 million ha) with total population of about 98 million. Minimum land area and population is observed in Maldives in South Asia and several Pacific Island countries.

The Agricultural Production Indices (1989-91 = 100, Gross Production of Agricultural Products) indicated (1995 data) that Myanmar ranked number one (141.9), followed by Iran (134.3), China (132.0) and Vietnam (124.3), very closely followed by Malaysia, India and Republic of Korea.

Rice is the most predominant crop of the region, China has the maximum production followed by India, Indonesia, Bangladesh, Thailand and Myanmar. The lowest records being from Papua New Guinea, Fiji and Bhutan. The region of Asia-Pacific recorded the highest production of rice, which compared safely with the total world production. Wheat is the next in rank. In case of its production, China ranked first followed by India and Pakistan in the Asia-Pacific region. Majority of the other countries in Northeast and South-East Asia and also Pacific Islands do not grow wheat except Mongolia and Myanmar. The Asia-Pacific region is again the largest producer of this crop. As regards maize, China is the largest producer followed by India, Indonesia, and Thailand. Highest annual growth rate (1985-1995) has been recorded by Papua New Guinea (9.9 per cent), Laos, (7.7 per cent), Vietnam (6.4 per cent), China and Malaysia (5.2 per cent). Among smaller countries in South Asia, Bhutan has shown appreciably higher growth rate (4.9 per cent). India and

Indonesia indicated 4.2 and 4.5 per cent annual growth rate, respectively. The region on the whole showed good growth rate as compared to rest of the world.

The production of millets, India ranked first followed by China, Myanmar, Nepal and Pakistan, none of the countries of South-East Asia and Pacific Islands grow millets. For the overall cereal production, China ranked first, followed by India, Indonesia, Bangladesh, Pakistan, Thailand, Vietnam and Myanmar. Again, the Asia-Pacific region is the largest producer of total cereal crops in the world. Among the root and tuberous crops (Cassava, yams and taros), China ranks number one, closely followed by India, Thailand, Indonesia, and Vietnam. Besides most of the countries of Pacific Islands, Bangladesh and Sri Lanka in South Asia sub-region also grow these crops.

Among the pulse crops, taking into account area and production, China ranked number one followed by India, Myanmar and Pakistan. Further Bangladesh, Thailand and Vietnam also cultivated considerable area under pulses whereas in terms of overall production, India ranked first followed by China and Myanmar. Among other countries of Asia, Pakistan and Bangladesh also recorded good production. The maximum annual growth rate (1985-1995) was recorded for Myanmar (7.8 per cent) and Laos (5.9 per cent) whereas India showed low annual growth rate (1.6 per cent). In overall perspective, the Asia-Pacific region recorded highest total pulse production. In terms of oil-crops production, China stood first, followed by Malaysia, India, Indonesia, Philippines, Thailand and Pakistan. In the Asia-Pacific region, Maldives, Indonesia, Laos, India, Malaysia, Thailand, Combodia, and Vietnam, have recorded high annual growth rate in terms of production of oil crops. The region produced almost half of the world production and indicated very high annual growth rate (5 per cent) as compared to the world average of 3.4 per cent.

The Asia-Pacific region also indicated almost half of the production of major fruit crops, excluding melons, with an average annual growth of 4.7 per cent. China ranked first in overall production followed by India, Iran, Indonesia, Philippines and Vietnam. Other major tropical fruit producing countries are Bangladesh, Malaysia, DPR Korea, Pakistan, Myanmar, Papua New Guinea, Republic of Korea and Sri Lanka. Besides, Australia, Japan and New Zealand are the major developed countries producing both tropical and temperate fruits. Major banana producing countries in the region are India, China, Philippines, Indonesia, Thailand, Vietnam, Bangladesh, Malaysia and Papua New Guinea and the production is substantial. The Asia-Pacific region again produces almost half of the total banana production with an annual growth rate of 3.5 per cent.

For *Citrus* group of fruits, China is the largest producer followed by India, Iran, Pakistan, Thailand and Republic of Korea. Besides Indonesia, Philippines and Vietnam have also recorded substantial production. Other countries of Pacific region are small producers. Among developed countries, Japan is number one followed by Australia. Overall picture showed that the Asia-Pacific region produced almost one-fourth of the total world production with an average annual growth rate of 5.3 per cent.

A large number of countries grow sugarcane in the region. Among these, India ranks number one, and stands just behind Indonesia in overall yield. China is number two in production followed by Thailand, Pakistan, Indonesia, Vietnam and Bangladesh. Among Pacific Island countries, Fiji is the largest producer and in terms of yields it ranks eighth in the region. Australia and Japan are also good producers with appreciably very high yields. The region accounts for almost half of the world sugarcane production with an average annual growth rate of 4.0 per cent.

Global Issues, Debates and International Efforts

In the past, free exchange (unrestricted) of germplasm, new crop species and elite strains from one country to another, and from one continent to another particularly from centres of origin and diversity to other regions/countries, contributed significantly towards the agricultural transformation, diversification and economic development. Introduction and migration of plant species played a very crucial and important role in diversification of food and other products. For example, wheat originated in the near east region but became an important cereal crop the world over. Rice, particularly *indica* types originated in South and South-East Asian region are cultivated even in far off countries such as the United States, which has become one of the largest producers. Maize, beans and potato from the Central American region, became important crop in countries of Europe, Asia and Africa. Soyabean, originating in Manchuria (Sino-Japanese region) is now most predominant crop in the United States. Similarly, sunflower (*Helianthus annus*) and other allied species from North America have become very prominent oilseed crop in Russia, several east European and Asian countries. Sweet Potato, pineapple, cassava, taros, tomato, capsicum chilly, cashew, coffee, tea, rubber and oilpalm, all represent excellent examples of free flow of germplasm exchange. The economy of several countries has grown mainly due to such unrestricted flow of germplasm. Almost every country of the world has benefited immensely without exception. Green revolution witnessed in Asian countries illustrates the advantage and the benefit that may have accrued from such free exchange of germplasm.

The Convention on Biological Diversity (CBD) held at Rio de Janeiro, Brazil in June 1992 and signed by 168 countries, for the first time recognized the sovereign rights of states (country) on its natural resources including plant genetic resources. However, several important issues such as 'access to plant genetic resources', 'benefit sharing' arising out of the use of plant genetic resources, 'farmer's rights' and rights of indigenous people — their knowledge, innovations and practices, realms of biotechnology, biosafety, transfer of technology etc. remained unresolved. Further, several new issues such as Breeders Rights, Intellectual Property Rights (IPR) and Trade Related Intellectual Property Rights (TRIPS) emerged with the signing of GATT and WTO. These developments had serious consequences and implications that further complicated the free exchange of germplasm.

Meeting of Conference of Parties (COP) held at Nairobi, Kenya in November, 1993 requested the FAO Commission on Plant Genetic Resources to revise its FAO Undertaking on Plant Genetic Resources through negotiations in order to harmonize it with Convention on Biological Diversity (CBD). Since then efforts have been made by FAO Commission on Plant Genetic Resources for its revisions. FAO brought out an important document on "World Status of Plant Genetic Resources" and also developed a Global Plan of Action (GPA) based on 20 major activities related to conservation and sustainable utilization of germplasm. The Fourth Technical Conference on Plant Genetic Resources, held at Leipzig, Germany in June, 1996 also emphasize on a constructive and concrete action with adequate technical and financial support encouraging activities on conservation and better utilization of plant genetic resources.

The institutional mechanisms provided by the FAO's intergovernmental Commission on Plant Genetic Resources for Food and Agriculture and the Convention on Biological Diversity (CBD) for the conservation and sustainable use of biological (genetic) resources are supplementary to each other and provide suggestive and legal options, respectively. The recognition of genetic resources away from the heritage of mankind and as sovereign resource of countries (parties) by the CBD have also brought in elements of benefits sharing arising out from use of biological diversity and equity. Eventually, the need to think of lasting solutions for issues like food security, sustainable natural resource management, equity, social justice, diversification in agriculture and global competitiveness, has been felt more than before. The instrument of mutual collaboration was, therefore, explored by national agricultural research systems in different regions and, as a result, the regional fora, such as the APAARI, have emerged. Further, in order to revisit priorities for agricultural research and to meet growing demand for food in the developing countries, the Global Plan of Action (GPA) has been adopted at Leipzig in 1996. The region provided a platform to collectively prioritize research needs and agenda for collaboration. Such efforts have only supplemented in undertaking appropriate research to solve the complex problems faces by countries, establishing new research paradigms involving national research institutes in order to meet the overall challenges. Asia-Pacific Consultation on Plant Genetic Resources held at New Delhi in November 1996 dealt on several important issue in this direction.

In the recent time, the economic policies have shifted from being inward to outward looking and most of the countries in the Asia-pacific region are becoming fully integrated to the global market. With an outward looking policy, it has become imperative for the NARS in the region to strive for greater efficiency to achieve global competitiveness in the agricultural production and marketing. The need has become more important with the membership of these countries to the World Trade Organization (WTO). The economic liberalization provides newer opportunities for enhancing and diversifying trade. With the development of Asian Free Trade Agreements (AFTA), the GATT and an increased membership of APAARI, the forum has already taken several catalytic measures, including increased communication with members and others through its publications. Besides, APAARI through its medium term perspective Plan has enhanced the scope of better linkages on policy issues particularly in the regional and global context.

There is a need to identify NARS' individual strengths and those which are likely to be acquired in common to serve the regional interests of conservation and sustainable use of biological diversity, particularly the PGR. Harmonizing the activities related to research, education, and extension shall, therefore, be relevant and meaningful. The future agriculture is likely to be far more knowledge demanding due to emergence of several diverse, advance technologies, including the biotechnologies and genetic engineering. Therefore, higher skills of management, healthy competition, and collaborative, mission-mode projects would essentially provide impetus to the pace of conservation and development. The proposed plan of action includes strengthening of the weaker NARS and building up NARS-NARS partnership in agricultural research, securing financial support for need based priority projects as per the regional needs and in accordance with the global plan of action. CGOAR has also emphasized the need to simultaneously address both the research priorities and the modalities for action. It is opined that the eco-regional programmes are well suited to such collaborations and thus be adopted as envisaged in the recommendations of the Asia-Pacific Regional Consultation on Plant Genetic Resources.

Priorities of CG Centres and other IARCs for the Asia-Pacific Region

Consultative Group on International Agriculture Research (CGIAR) and International Agricultural Research Centres (IARCs), which operate under the auspices of CGIAR, closely co-operate and work with National Agricultural Research Systems (NARS). Ninety per cent of rice is grown in the region of Asia-Pacific (IRRI mandate). IRRI's ecosystem approach to rice research had 4 areas; upland rice, rainfed rice, irrigated rice, and flood prone rice and the Centre's future emphasis will be more on rainfed areas. However, future targets for impact shall include both irrigated and rainfed types. The new research paradigms to achieve the targets include systems approach, use of new research techniques to reduce research costs (crop models, GIS, etc.), and farmer-participatory adaptive research. The latter has an important bearing both on the sustainability and on farm conservation. Major portion of area and production of ICRISAT's mandate crops are also located in this region. This is likely to have a definite bearing on Centre's research priorities. One third of the CIMMYT's resources are spent in Asia to develop sustainable maize and wheat production systems. Main emphasis is focused on reducing genetic vulnerability and increasing sustainability of production. At the same time, it is urgent to prioritize research on rice-wheat systems, which are the backbone of agriculture in South Asia and also parts of South-East Asia. Strengthening activities of the Rice-Wheat Consortium, is therefore important. ICARDA's global mandate is to improve the welfare of people in dry areas and regional mandate on chickpea, bread wheat, durum wheat besides lentil, barley, faba bean and farming systems, whereas irrigation efficiency and conservation of water resources are the main themes of IWMI. The latter has developed a climate and water atlas of the world on CD-ROM which is of immediate use to NARS and for further research.

ICLARM addresses food security in world, focusing on low-income people. APAARI has been considered by the NARS as well as CG Centres as a catalyst and also a bridge. More emphasis is being laid on increased linkages among NARS and the CG Centres through APAARI. Also, the networks are being foreseen to play a major role, especially in biodiversity conservation, germplasm enhancement, training and information exchange.

ILRI's global mandate is to improve animal performance, conserve biodiversity, sustainable livestock systems, animal health improvement, and strengthening NARS. Priorities and activities are identified in consultation with partners in different regions and globally. Current activities include assessing the status of animal agriculture in Asia, and livestock improvement in upland farming systems in South-East Asia. CIP concentrates on potato and sweet potato. Its role is foreseen in developing/ strengthening network on CIP's mandate crops in the region, which is considered important. The AVRDC is an Asia based institute, laying 60-70 per cent emphasis on activities related to the region. Its mandate includes emphasis for improved nutrition, farm income, and environmental sustainability using vegetables and it caters to three sub-regional research networks : AVNET (South-East Asia), CLVNET (Indo-China), SAVERNET (South Asia).

CABI, an inter-governmental, mission oriented, bioscience organization located in Australia has 40 member countries, with good representation from Asia-Pacific region. It assists in sustainable development by information dissemination. Its partnership with APAARI and member countries is foreseen to enhance research relevance, quality and impact.

Research Priorities of the Asia-Pacific Region

The recommendations endorsed by APAARI for prioritizing areas of agricultural research in the region include the following :

- Major crop/commodity research areas : Rice, wheat, maize, mungbean, soyabean, tropical vegetable, plantation crops, cattle, buffalo, piggery, poultry, fisheries.
- System approach : Rice-Wheat production systems, Farming Systems Research, Agro-Forestry Land Use Systems.
- Socioeconomic research and policy-planning.
- Support to centres of excellence around the component NARS institutes/scientists and strengthening of smaller NARS for effective management through human resource development.
- Strengthening Regional coordination activities, information management system and networks.
- Biodiversity conservation management, germplasm enhancement and use.
- Use of Biotechnology in agriculture and biosafety.
- Post-harvest management, processing on future scenario for agriculture and agri-business in the Asia-Pacific region, looking ahead for the next decade and beyond.

Agro-Biodiversity Management Issues/Concerns

The issue that nations should have their own policy on genetic resources is being strongly influenced by the several international developments, such as, the Convention on Biological Diversity, its Conference of Parties (COP) and the

Subsidiary Body for Scientific, Technical and Technological Matters (SBSTTA); the Trade Related Intellectual Property Rights (TRIPS); the Sanitary and Phyto Sanitary Agreements (SPS) in the World Trade Organization (WHO) and the Breeder's Rights in the Union of Protection of New Plant Species (UPOV). Accordingly, it is seen that the FAO Commission on Plant Genetic Resources that served as a torchbearer to the global community in the broad area of food production, agriculture and development since eighties has undergone sea changes in terms of its policies and priorities. These include a revised nomenclature [FAO Commission on Genetic Resources for Food and Agriculture (CGRFA)] to include animal genetic resources and others in its folds, the adoption of the Global Plan of Action (GPA) and the revision of International Undertaking on Plant Genetic Resources.

The broader areas that got affected include the intellectual property regime, the access to biological resources, the sharing of benefits and equity. The status of awareness in different countries in the region varies considerably and some appropriate measures are taken/being taken in the Philippines, India and other countries. In India, such measures being taken to cope up with the emerging situation include drafting of a Plant Variety Protection and Farmers' Rights Act, a Biological Diversity Act and the formulation of National Action Plan for biological diversity conservation. The Public Sector institutions and the non-governmental organizations are taking a joint lead in attempting to flag and resolve issues of concern. In India, the Indian Society of Plant Genetic Resources (ISPGR) in collaboration with NBPGR made a serious effort and organized it first dialogue in 1993 on plant genetic resources — Developing National Policy Options. It came out with very useful recommendations. Such concern on agro-biodiversity management, conservation and use was jointly addressed by various stockholders with the efforts of National Academy of Agricultural Sciences and the Indian Council of Agricultural Research in October, 1997 at Shimla. The scientists' perception was crystallized to draw out some useful recommendations that need follow-up in the country and may also be applicable in the region with suitable changes to meet individual country's requirements. The deliberations resulted in some constructive recommendations that are briefly dealt here.

It is important that all action henceforth, on the conservation related issues should be based on well founded national action plan of the individual country and that such plans must give due emphasis on collaboration, capacity building and human resource development. The agro-biodiversity and the available indigenous knowledge is important to each country in its own right which should be documented on priority in a well organized approach. Both formal and informal knowledge available with the farming communities is important. This should be retrieved by appropriate means and methodologies, and documented. It is also important that the peace of collection and conservation of agro-biodiversity be accelerated to avoid any further inadvertent losses. At the same time, it is important to ensure that the collections are conserved, secure and safe. What is conserved must be protected with the respective country's own efforts or with the help of other well developed national programmes, CC Centres, FAO or other regional/international bodies which have such expertise, competence and capabilities in securing adequate financial support for the specific mission. A high priority needs to be accorded to different researchable topics related to agro-biodiversity management and use. This could be pursued through action of the National Agricultural Research System (NARS) involving the various stockholder, such as, the NCOs, the private sector and the farming communities and through the active support of the FAO.

The agro-biodiversity conservation is a high priority activity which could be achieved through a judicious admixture of both *ex situ* and *in situ* approaches. China and India already hold large germplasm collections among the largest genebanks in the world whereas some smaller island countries face the basic problems of seed storage for even medium to short term. A regional approach and the APAARI mediated NARS-NARS collaborations could be envisaged in the larger interest of germplasm conservation. However, the genuine concern of sustaining huge genebanks has to be voiced by the regional fora to safeguard the interests of their member countries. Pending creation of a Biological Diversity Fund and a lean support by the CEF for the said purpose, the regional countries need to come forward for closer co-operation and international agencies should assure need based support.

Conservation technologies for the non-orthodox seed species and vegetatively propagated crop plants, particularly medicinal and aromatic plants and other high value crops, have to be developed with innovations and appropriate indigenous, cheaper technology. The needed support for research in such cases may be provided by interested donors in different countries and at various institutions with defined responsibilities. Furthermore, *in situ* on farm conservation should be promoted wherever feasible. An effective *in situ* on farm conservation of traditional cultivars/ landrace, and farming systems may be sometimes suitable across the political boundaries and wherever such opportunities exist the same should be pursued. APAARI could undertake feasibility studies, work out communities and the exclusive elements so that some NARS-APAARI collaborations may pursue for action under the global plan. Specific areas, practices, systems and species have to be identified and case studies with common denominators can be approved by/through APAARI for making a suitable database. National systems are required to be evolved to find out farmers' views and expectations towards sustainable *in situ* on farm conservation of genetic diversity. And, in this context, modes and mechanisms of providing appropriate incentives or suitable compensation/incentives to farmers need to be evolved so as to arouse farmer's interest and ensure safe conservation of genetic resources.

The importance of ethnic groups, the womenfolk and their role in the conservation of traditional varieties, especially in fragile and vulnerable agro-ecosystems is duly recognized. It must be further added that the ethnic and gender issues cannot be separated from the mission of conservation and thus reward and compensation mechanisms are inseparable rather congruent with the on form conservation strategies, which must address these at large. Some experiments on pilot scale, taken up with the aim to develop suitable conservation model(s) *in situ* on farm conservation should include the gender, ethnic and eco-regional dimensions. Also emphasis should be laid to identify indicator species in order to assess the health of different agro-ecosystems and sub-systems. It is pertinent to include conservation of available breeds/strains of animals, fish and microbes in the on farm conservation models. Destruction is easy, re-building is difficult and particularly more so if the precedences are lost. Therefore a collective yet decentralized approach may be developed to address the common elements of agro-biodiversity from different plant kingdoms and phyla.

Simple and sustained bio-prospecting of agro-biodiversity and its moniting are important components at the grassroot level of the systematic *in situ* — on farm agro-biodiversity management. This area needs to be resolved, used appropriate protocol and by involving amateurs and local folk. The genetic variability of native underutilized species of food crops, fruits, medicinal and aromatic, and other economic plants needs to be documented on priority. Need based introduction of useful species in problem areas shall, however, remain the best option. Some of the selective, hitherto unexploited species having future potential may be researched and adopted by individual NARS and their success stories can be shared on the regional platform through APAARI.

A consciousness is alive to the urgent need for appropriate quarantine measures across the political boundaries. Countries must revisit their National Plant Quarantine Policies, particularly in the context of bio-engineered materials/genetically modified organisms (GMO) and capacity-building addressed jointly so that the fear of widening gaps between Developed-Developing world relationships on the issue of markets for transgenics is resolved and appropriate precautionary measures are taken timely.

PGR conservation alone has little meaning unless suitably linked to sustainable use. Characterization evaluation and documentation of these resources, therefore, deserves a high priority. Deployment of improved tools and technologies, such as biotechnology, is expensive and so far exclusive, but it should receive more attention in a collaborative mode particularly for training and HRD in favour of weaker NARS. Improving the communication links through information networks and databases on germplasm is also required to be strengthened. APAARI is well poised to look forward to the joint strength of its members, associate members and other interest groups in the region.

Considering the specific relevance of agro-biodiversity in the emerging global scenario, there is a need to create awareness and understanding among the masses. Governments may encourage it through literacy campaign for conservation and sustainable management of agro-biodiversity, beginning from the primary level of education. Similarly, non-governmental organizations with appropriate patronage of the respective NARS should disseminate this knowledge at the grassroot level. Emphasis should be laid on human resource development to build required expertise in basic PGR management aspects, namely, identification, germplasm collection, characterization, evaluation, documentation and conservation. At the same time, the reorientation for technology generation would be helpful. The HRD should, therefore, be further oriented towards the needed expertise, technology and awareness for germplasm management, regeneration and conservation, including on-farm conservation.

The issues of access and benefit are intricate and sensitive; hence, these need due focus. We may learn from others' experiences or set our own precedence but must address these willfully and with the needed thrust. A well understood procedure for accessing the genetic resource materials owned by farming communities/individuals and a fair and equitable sharing of profits arising out of their use should be established. The revenue generated through benefit sharing could be consolidated and transferred to a specific fund to be made exclusively available for research and development relating to public good and/or for the community development activities. Sharing the materials among community/national seed banks, researchers and other users is undeniably required. This could be pursued with suitable MOUs agreements or other legal commitments. It is ultimately desirable in the national, regional and global interests. A fair and equitable mechanism developed by/for all stockholders would alone safeguard the interests of all concerned.

Nations may constitute policy advisory committees on matters concerning agro-biodiversity conservation and related issues. The legislation could also be developed so that effective instruments are made available for conservation, management and use. The region is well poised in the gene rich segment of the globe and requires further interaction with the developed world, on new technologies. Required institutional support and the human resource needed for generating improved technolgoies should, however, be developed within the region on priority. This would help in addressing problems of common dimensions, such as a *sui generis* system for each member country to protect agro-biodiversity, through both innovative and scientific approaches, and addressing, all possible social, political and legal issues.

8

Ecology and Technological Changes

IN THE dominant paradigm, technology is seen as being above society both in its structure and in evolution, in its offering technological fixes, and in its technological determinism. It is seen as a source of solution to problems that lie in society, and is rarely perceived as a source of new social problems. Its course is viewed as being self-determined. In periods of rapid technological transformation, it is assumed that society and people must adjust to that change, instead of technological change adjusting to the social values of equity sustainability and participation.

There is, however, another perspective which treats technological change as a process that is shaped by and serves the priorities of whomever controls it. In this perspective, a narrow social base of technological choice excludes human concerns and public participation. The interests of that base are protected in the name of sustaining an inherently progressive and socially neutral technology. On the other hand, a broader social base protects human rights and the environment by widening the circle of control beyond the current small group.

The emergence of the new biotechnologies brings out these two tendencies dramatically. The technocratic approach to biotechnology portrays the evaluation of the technology as self-determined and views social sacrifice as a necessity. Human rights including people's right to livelihoods therefore must be sacrificed for property rights that give protection to the innovation processes. Ironically, a process based on sacrifice of human rights continues to be projected as automatically leading to human well-being.

The sacrifice of people's rights to create new property rights is not new. It has been part of the hidden history of the rise of capitalism and its technological structures. The laws of private property which arose during the fifteenth and sixteenth centuries simultaneously eroded people's common rights to the use of forests and pastures while creating the social conditions for capital accumulation through industrialisation. The new laws of private property were aimed at protecting individual rights to property as a commodity, while destroying collective rights to commons as a basis of sustenance. The Latin root of private property, private, means 'to deprive'. The shift from human rights to private property rights is therefore a general social and political precondition for exclusivity technologies to take root in society. The scene for such a shift is now being set to allow the emergence of a biotechnological era of corporate and industrial growth.

In the narrow view, science and technology are conventionally accepted as what scientists and technologies produce, and development is accepted as what science and technology produce. Scientists and technologists are in turn taken to be that sociological category formally trained in Western Science and technology, either in institutions or organisations in the West, or in 'institutions mimicing the paradigms of the West. These definitions are unproblematic if one leaves our people, especially poor people, if one ignores cultural diversity and distinct civilisational histories of our planet which has created diverse and distinctive cultures. Development in this view is taken as synonymous with the introduction of Western Science and Technology in non-Western contexts. The magical identity is development = modernisation = Westernisation.

In a wider context where, science is viewed as 'ways of knowing' and technology as 'ways of doing' all societies, in all their diversity, have had science and technology systems on which their distinct and diverse development has been based. Technologies or systems of technologies bridge the gap between nature's resources and human needs. Systems of knowledge and culture provide the framework for the perception of definition of science and technology — science and technology are no longer viewed as uniquely Western but as a plurality association with all cultures and civilisations. And a particular science and technology do not automatically translate into development everywhere. Ecologically and economically inappropriate science and technology can become causes of underdevelopment, not solutions to underdevelopment. Ecological inappropriateness is a mismatch between the ecological processes of nature which renew life support systems and the resource demands and impact of technological processes. Technological processes can lead to higher withdrawals of natural resources or higher additions of pollutants that ecological limits allow. In such cases they contribute to underdevelopment through destruction of ecosystems.

Economic inappropriateness is the mismatch between the needs of society and the requirements of a technological system. Technological processes create demands for raw materials and markets, and control over both raw materials and markets becomes an essential part of the politics of technological change.

The lack of the theoretical cognition of the two ends of technological processes, its beginning in natural resources and its end in basic human needs, has created the current paradigm for economic and technological development which demands increasing withdrawals of natural resources and generates increasing addition of pollutants while marginalising and dispossessing increasing numbers from the productive process. These characteristics of contemporary scientific industrial development are the primary causes for the contemporary ecological, political and economic crises. The combination of ecologically disruptive scientific and technological modes and the absence of criteria for evaluating scientific and technological systems in terms of resource use efficiency and capability for basic needs satisfaction has created conditions where society is increasingly propelled towards ecological and economic instability and has no rational and organised response to arrest and curtail these destructive tendencies.

The introduction of ecological and economically inappropriate science and technology leads to underdevelopment instead of development. Modernisation based on resource hungry processes materially deprives communities which use those resources for survival, either directly, or through their ecological function. Growth under these conditions does not ensure development for all. It creates underdevelopment for these affected negatively by resource diversion or destruction. Conflicting demands on resources thus lead to economic polarisation through growth. The growing extent of the people's ecology movements is a symptom of this polarisation and reminds that natural resources play a vital role in the survival of the people. Their diversion to other uses or their destruction through other uses is therefore creating increasing impoverishment and an increasing threat to survival.

Underdevelopment is commonly projected as a state issue created by the absence of modern western science and technology systems. However, poverty and underdevelopment are, more often than not, conditions created by the externalised and invisible costs of resource intensive and resource destructive technological processes which support the livelihood of millions.

The experience of all industrial revolutions illustrates how poverty and underdevelopment is created as an integral part of the whole process of contemporary growth and development in which gains accrue to one section of the society or nation and the costs, economic or ecological are borne by the rest.

The first industrialisation was based on the mechanisation of work, with focus on the textile industry. The second industrialisation was based on the chemicalisation of processes in agriculture and other sectors, and the emerging third industrialisation is based on the engineering of life processes.

We can draw some lessons from history about how technological change initiated by a special interest brings development to that interest group while creating underdevelopment for others.

Colonisation and the Spinning Wheel

The mechanisation of textile manufacture was the leading technological transformation of the first industrial revolution. By the time that technological innovations made full impact on the British textile industry in the early 19th century, England had gained full political control over resources and its markets of its colonies; including India. India until then had been a leading producer and exporter of textiles in the world market. The industrialisation of England was based in part on the deindustrialisation of India. The development of England was based on India's underdevelopment. It is no co-incidence that India's independence movement was based in large measure on seeking liberation from the control on resources and people of Third World that were part of the process of Europe's industrialisation. Two symbols of India's independence struggle were the 'Champaran Satyagraha' and the 'Charkha'. The Champaran Satyagraha was a peaceful revolt against the forced cultivation of indigo as a dye for the British textile industry. The 'Charkha' or spinning wheel was the technological alternative that created self-reliance instead of dependence, and generated livelihoods instead of destroying them.

While the rapid technological innovations in the British textiles industry were made possible only through the prior control over the resources and the market, the stagnation and decay of this industry in India was a result of the loss of political control first over the market and later over the raw material. The destruction of India's textile industry necessitated the destruction of the skills and autonomy of India's weavers. Often this destruction was extremely violent. For instance, the thumbs of the West Bengal weavers were to cut off market competition when Indian had woven textiles continued to do better than the British mill products. The impact of the violence manipulation and control of the English merchants on the Indian weavers started when the East India Company became a territorial power by defeating Nawab Sirajuddaula in the battle of Palassi in 1757. Before that the Indian weavers were independent producers and had control over their produce. The East India company replaced the indigenous merchants by a 'body of paid servants receiving instructions from them with coercive authority over weavers that none had before. They had virtual monopoly of the market and had effectively exercised control over raw materials and began to extend this control over the weavers' tools. Under the company weavers had virtually become wage workers on terms and conditions over which they had no control.'

In the context of such erosion of the control on resources and the market, the traditional weavers of India were displaced, there was an exodus out of the weaving trade. New textile Technology was imported into India from England in the mid-19th century by the cotton traders of India who were involved in export of cotton to England. This new group of powerful merchants turned mill owners competed with the handloom weavers for the common market and the raw material base. The establishment of textile mills in Lancashire and later in India deprived the Indian weaver both of the market and the raw material. When the American cotton supply to the English textile industry was disturbed by the American civil war, the famous cotton famine of 1960s broke out and the English instantly reacted by grabbing the cotton in India. The cotton famine was transferred to India.

There was also a devastating impact of the new textile mills opened in India on the handloom weavers.

> "The growth of the industry began to impinge on the handloom industry.... This incursion of mills into areas hitherto considered the special reserves of the handloom industry had a many sided effect...and led to unprecedented worsening of the conditions of the handloom weavers.... Actual unemployment was seen as in the statistics of idle handlooms; this was estimated at 13 per cent in 1940 by the fact finding committee (of Handlooms and mills)."

Gandhi's critique of the industrialisation of India on the western model was based on his perception of the poverty, dispossession and destruction of livelihoods which resulted from it.

'Why must India become industrial in the western sense?' Gandhi has asked 'what is good for one nation situated in one condition is not necessarily good for another differently situated. One man's food is often another man's poison.... Mechanisation is good when hands are too few for the work intended to be accomplished. It is an evil where there are more hands than required for the work as is the case in India.'

It was to regenerate livelihoods in India that Gandhi thought of the spinning wheel as a symbol of liberation and a tool for development. Power driven mills were the model of development in that period of early industrialisation. However, the hunger of mills for raw-material and markets was the reason for a new poverty, created by the destruction of livelihoods either by diverting land and biomass from local subsistence to the factory, or by displacing local production through the market.

Gandhi had said that 'anything that millions can do together, becomes charged with unique power. The spinning wheel had become a symbol of such power. The wheel as such is lifeless, but when I invest it with symbolism, it becomes a living thing for me.'

When Gandhi described the Charkha in 1908, in Hind-Swaraj as a panacea for the growing pauperism of India, he had never seen a spinning wheel. Even in 1915, when he returned to India from South Africa, he had not actually seen a spinning wheel. But he saw an essential element of freedom from colonialism in discarding the use of mill woven cloth. He set up handlooms in the Satyagraha Ashram at Sabarmati, but could not find a spinning wheel or a spinner, who were normally women. In 1917, Gandhi's disciple Gangabehn Majumdar started a search for the spinning wheel, and found one in Vijapur in the Baroda State. Quite a few people there had spinning wheels in their homes, but had long since consigned them to the lofts as useless lumbers. They now pulled them out, and soon Vijapur Khadi gained a name for itself. And Khadi and the spinning wheel rapidly become the symbol for India's independence movement.

The spinning wheel symbolised a technology that conserves resources, people's livelihoods and people's control over their livelihoods. In contrast to the imperialism of the British textile industry, the 'Charkha' was decentred and labour generating, not labour displacing. It need people's hands and minds, instead of treating them as surplus, or as mere inputs into an industrial process. This critical mixture of decentralisation, livelihood generation, resources conservation and strengthening of self-reliance were essential to undo the waste of centralisation, livelihood destruction, resource depletion and creation of economic and political dependence that had been engendered by the industrialisation association with colonialism.

Gandhi's spinning wheel is a challenge to notions of progress and obsolescence that arise from absolutism and false universalism in concepts of science and technology development. Obsolescence and waste are social constructs that have both a political and ecological component. Politically, the notion of obsolescence gets rid of people's control over their lives and livelihoods by defining productive work as unproductive and removing peoples control over production in the name of progress. It would rather waste hands than waste time. Ecologically, to obsolescence destroys the regenerative capacity of nature by substituting manufactured uniformity in place of nature's diversity. This induced dispensability of poorer people on the one hand and diversity on the other constitutes of the political ecology of technological development guided by narrow and reductionist notions of productivity. Parochial notions of productivity, perceived as universal, rob people of control over their means of reproducing life and rob nature of her capacity to regenerate diversity.

Ecological erosion and destruction of livelihoods are linked to one another. Displacement of diversity and displacement of people's sources of sustenance both arise from a view of development and growth based on uniformity created through centralised control. In this process of control, reductionist science and technology act as handmaidens for economically powerful interests. The struggle between the factory and the spinning wheel continues as new technologies emerge.

The Colonisation of the Seed

The changes that took place in the textile industry during colonialism were replayed in agriculture after India's independence through the Green Revolution. Whether it was the chemicalisation of agriculture through the Green Revolution or its transformation through the new biotechnologies, the seed is at the centre of all recent changes in agricultural production. All technological transformation of biodiversity is justified in the language of 'improvement' and increase of 'economic value'. However, 'improvement' and 'value' are not neutral terms. They are contextual and value laden. What is improvement in one context is often regression in another. What is value added from one perspective is value lost from another.

The 'improvement' of the seed is not a neutral economic process. It is, more importantly a political process that shifts control over biological diversity from local peasants transnational systems reproducing themselves into raw material. It therefore changes the role of the agricultural producer and the role of ecological processes.

As Kloppenburg has stated

> "It decouples seed as 'seed' from seed as 'grain' and thereby facilitates the transformation of seed from a use-value to an exchange value."

Agricultural research is primarily a means of eliminating barriers to the penetration of agriculture by capital. The most important barrier is the nature of the seed, which reproduces itself and multiples. The seed thus possesses a dual character that links both ends of the process of crop production : It is both means of production and, as grain, the product. In planting each year's crop the farmers also reproduce a necessary part of their means of production. The seed thus presents capital with a simple biological obstacle : Given appropriate conditions the seed will reproduce itself manifold.

The seed has therefore to be transformed materially if a market for seed has to be created.

Modern plant breeding is primarily an attempt to remove this biological obstacle to the market in seed. Seed reproducing itself stays free, a common resource and under the farmers control. Corporate seed has a cost and is under the control of the corporate sector or under the control of agricultural research institutions. The transformation of a common resource into a commodity, of a self-regenerative resource into mere 'input' changes the nature of the seed and of agriculture itself. Since it robs peasants of their means of livelihood, the new technology becomes as instrument of poverty and underdeveloped.

The decoupling of seed from grain also changes the status of seed. From being a finished produce which rises from itself, nature's needs and people's seeds becomes mere raw material for the production of corporate seed as commodity. The cycle or regeneration of biodiversity is therefore replaced by a linear flow of free germ plasm from farms and forests into labs and research stations, and the flow of modified uniform products as priced commodities from corporations to farmers. Diversity is destroyed by transforming it into mere raw material for industrial production based on uniformity which necessarily displaces the diversity of local agricultural practice.

Cropping systems in general, involve an interaction between soil, water and plant genetic resources. In indigenous agriculture, for example, cropping systems include a symbiotic relationship between soil, water, farm animals and plants. Green Revolution agriculture replaces this integration at the level of the farm with the integration of inputs such as seeds and chemicals. The indigenous cropping systems are based only on internal organic inputs. Seeds come from the farm, soil fertility comes from the farm and pest control is built into the crop mixtures. In the Green Revolution package, yields are intimately led to purchase inputs of seeds chemical fertilizers, pesticides and petroleum and intensive irrigation. High yields are not intrinsic to the seeds, but are a function of the availability of inputs. The UNRISD (United Nations Research Institute of Social Developments) 15 nation study of the impact of the new seeds concluded the term High Yielding variety is a misnomer because it implies that the new seeds are high-yielding in and of themselves. The distinguishing feature of the seeds, however, is that they are highly responsive to certain key inputs such as fertilizer and irrigation. Palmer therefore suggested the term 'high-responsive varieties' (HRVs) in place of high yielding varieties (HYVs).

As Claude Alvares has said 'for the first time the human race has produced seed that cannot cope on its own, but needs to be placed within an artificial environment for growth and output'.

This change in the nature of seed is justified by creating a framework that treats self-regenerative seed as 'primitive' and as 'raw' germplasm, and the seed that is inert without inputs and non-reproducible, as a finished product. The whole is rendered partial, the partial is rendered whole. The commoditised seed is ecologically incomplete and ruptured at two levels :

(1) It does not reproduce itself, while by definition, seed is a re-generative resource. Genetic resources are thus, through technological transformation, transformed from a renewable into a non renewable.

(2) It does not produce by itself. It needs the help of inputs to produce. As the seed and chemical companies merge, the dependence on inputs will increase, not decrease. And ecologically whether a chemical is added externally or internally, it remains an external input in the ecological cycle of the reproduction of seed.

It is this shift the ecological processes of reproduction to the technological processes of production that underlies both the problem of dispossession of farmers and of genetic erosion.

The new plant biotechnologies will follow the path of the earlier HYV's of the Green Revolution in pushing farmers onto a technological treadmill. Biotechnology can be expected to increase the release of farmers on purchased inputs even as it accelerates the process of polarisation. It will even increase the use of chemicals instead of decreasing. The dominant focus of research in genetic engineering is not on fertilizer-free and pest-free crops, put pesticide and herbicide-resistant varieties. For the seed-chemical multinations, this might make commercial sense, since it is cheaper to adapt the plant to the chemical than to adopt the chemical to the plant. The cost of developing a new crop variety rarely reaches $ 2 million, whereas the cost of a new herbicide exceeds $ 40 million.

Herbicide and pesticide resistance will also increase the integration of seeds/chemicals and the multinationals' control of agriculture. A number of major agricultural-chemical companies are developing plants with resistance to their brand of herbicides. Soyabeans have been made resistant to Ciba-Geigy's Atrazin herbicides and this has increased annual sales of the herbicide by $ 120 million. Research is also being done to develop crop plants resistant to other herbicides, such as Dupont's 'Gist and Glean' and Monsanto's 'Round-UP', which are lethal to most herbaceous plants and thus cannot be applied directly to crops. The successful development and sale of crop plants resistant to brand-name herbicides will result in further economic concentration of the agriculture industry market, increasing the market power of transnational companies. The farmers will own the land, but the corporation will own the crop in the field, giving instructions by a computer that monitors the progress and needs of a crop grown from genetically programmed seed.

Biotechnology can thus become an instrument for dispossessing the farmer of seed, as a means of production. The relocation of seed production from the farm to the corporate lab relocates power and value between the North and South; and between corporations and farmers. It is estimated that the elimination of home grown seed would dramatically increase the farmer's dependence on biotech industries by about $ 6 billion annually.

It also becomes an instrument of dispossession by selectively removing those plants or parts of plants that do not serve the commercial interest but are essential for survival of nature and people. 'Improvement' of a selected characteristic in a plant, is also a selection against other characteristics which are useful to nature, or for local consumption. Improvement is not a class or gender neutral concept. Improvement of partitioning efficiency is based on the 'enhancement' of the yield of desired product at the expense of unwanted plant parts. The desired product is however, not the same for rich people and poor people, or rich countries and poor countries, nor is efficiency. On the input side, richer people and richer countries are short labour and poorer people and poorer countries are short of capital and land. Most agricultural development, however, increases capital input while displacing labour, thus destroying livelihoods. On the output side, which parts of a farming system of a plant will be treated as 'unwanted' for the better off may be the wanted part for the poor. The plants or 'plant parts' which serve the poor are the ones whose supply is squeezed by the normal priorities of improvement in response to commercial forces.

In the Indian context, plants that have been displaced by plant improvement in the Green Revolution are pulses and oilseeds, which are crucial to the nutrient needs of people and the soil. Monocultures of wheat and rice spread through the Green Revolution have also turned useful plants into weeds, as is the case with green leafy vegetables which grow as associates. Herbicides use has destroyed plants useful for the poor, pesticide use has destroyed the fish culture usually system. These losses through biodiversity destruction resulting from increasing yields of monocultures in never internalised in the productivity measure of technological change. Instead, both increased inputs and decreased outputs are externalised in measurement of productivity. Productivity is a measure of output per unit input. A typical subsistence farm in an Asian village produces more than twenty crops and supports animals. Individual crops are also multipurpose. Rice, for instance, is only partially food. The residue after the removal of the grain is not a nuisance to be disposed of as it would be on a farm in the developed world. The straw is used to feed animals, to cook food, or even to help fertilize the field for the next year's crops — the straw and husk are important construction material. Traditional rice varieties produced five times as much straw as grain, and were an important source of food, feed, fuel, fertilizer and housing material.

Plant breeders, however, saw rice only as food and created a science and technology to increase grain yields. Traditional crop varieties, characterised by tall and thin straw typically convert the heavy doses of fertilizers into overall growth of the plant rather than increasing the grain yield. Commonly, the excessive growth of the plant causes the stalk to break, lodging the grain on the ground, which results in heavy crop losses. The 'miracle seeds' or 'high yielding varieties' which started the process of the Green Revolution were biologically engineered to be dwarf varieties. The important feature of these new varieties is not that they are particularly productive in themselves but that they can absorb three or four times higher doses of fertilizer than the traditional varieties and convert it into grain, provided proportionately heavy and frequent irrigation applications are also available. They also have high susceptibility to insect and pest attacks.

For equivalent fertilization, the high yielding varieties produce about the same total biomass as the traditional rice. They increase the grain yield at the straw. Thus while traditional rice produces four to five times as much straw as grain, high yielding rice typically produce a one-to-one ratio of grain to straw. Thus a conversion from traditional to high yielding rice increases the grain available but decreases the straw. Abundance creates scarcity. Output as total biomass does not increase, but the input increases dramatically. High yielding varieties of wheat for example need about three times as much irrigations as traditional varieties. If water is considered as a critical output, the productivity of the new seeds is only a third of the productivity of traditional varieties. In terms of water use, the green revolution is clearly counter-productive. Increased irrigation intensity has future costs associated with it in water logging and salinity, as the experience in India's Punjab has shown. In other regions such as Maharashtra and Tamil Nadu, the Green Revolution is causing large scale of ground water. Large scale dessication of the regions of the world now supporting the green revolution is thus a real possibility. Abundance again generates scarcity.

The increased water, fertilizer, and pesticide use is also counter-productive for the Asian farmer in financial terms. From studies conducted at the International Rice Research Institute, it is estimated that whereas the total cash costs of production for the average Filipino rice farmer using traditional methods and varieties is about $ 20 per hectare, the cost rises to $ 220 when the new high yielding varieties are grown.

The fragmentation of components of the farm ecosystem and their integration with distant markets and industries is a characteristic of modern 'scientific' agriculture. The most common justification of the introduction of this system of food production is that it raises agricultural productivity. The high 'productivity' of modern agriculture is however a myth when total resource inputs are taken into account. The social and ecological costs with respect to the manufacture and use of fertilizers, pesticides and labour replacing energy and equipment are never taken into account, thus rendering the system artificially productive. If the energy used to provide all inputs to modern farming agricultural technologies are found to be counterproductive. Whereas the turn of the century even in the countries of the North, one calorie of food value was produced by the input of less than a calorie of energy so that there was a net gain, today ten calories of energy are used to produce the same one calorie of food value.

The higher productivity and efficiency of industrial agricultural is contextually determined, by selecting those inputs and output which suit the endowments of rich people and rich countries. Before we push through new agricultural technologies, it would be wise to pause and look at the other paths that were available for increased production but were never considered. Alternatives in agriculture have been based on conserving nature and people livelihoods, while improving yields, not on destroying them.

The myth that only chemically intensive labour displacing agriculture is productive has recently been challenged by a major study of the National Research Council in the U.S. The report, titled 'Alternative Agriculture' shows that besides reducing the health and environmental hazards posed by chemical agriculture, alternative farming systems have economic viability. Traditionally, most evaluations comparing chemical farming to alternative practices have focussed principally on the cost and returns of adopting a specific farming method. Fewer studies have considered the impact of alternative farming systems on the economic performance of the whole farm. The committee could find no useful studies of the potential effects of widespread adoption of alternative agricultural systems. And the committee could find no aggregate studies to compare the cost and benefits of conventional agriculture with successful alternative systems. Most studies have the flawed approach of comparing the conventional farming practices with the economic performance of a similar farm, assuming withdrawal of certain categories of farm inputs instead of comparison with farm with alternatives. The bias in favour of Green Revolution and chemical agriculture has distorted the assessment and potential of alternative agriculture. However, the new search for alternatives is showing that sustainable farming systems do not have to compromise at the level of productivity and yields.

A case study of the Thompson Farm established yields of 130-150 bushels/acre for corn against the national average of 124 bushels/acre, 44-55 bushels/acre of soyabean against the national average of 40 bushels/acre and 4-5 tonnes/acre of hay against 3-4 tonnes/acre of the national average. Similarly at the Kitamira farm, the yields of 35.5 tonnes/acre of tomatoes was much high than the country's average.

It is not only countries like US which are making a shift away from energy and chemical intensive agriculture. In India, a decade long experiment with 'rishi kheti' or alternative agriculture undertaken at Friends Rural Centre in Rasulia, Madhya Pradesh by Pratap Aggarwal yielded higher returns with indigenous seeds and no external inputs than the Green Revolution agriculture of HYV seeds and heavy chemical and irrigation inputs which had been earlier practised on the farm.

In the terai-region of Uttar Pradesh a local farmer called Inder Singh continued to grow traditional varieties while most farmers shifted to a HYV called Pant-4. As intensive irrigation led to a decline in the water table, the thirsty HYVs could no longer be cultivated. Inder Singh's seeds came in useful. Owing to high productivity and low costs of cultivation in terms of fertilizer and water input, a particular variety called Indarasan (named after water Indar Singh) spread to cover nearly 50 per cent of the area. During drought years, Indarasan has coped much better than Pant-4 with yields of 32 quintals per acre compared to Pant-4 which has stagnated at 20 quintals per acre under irrigation. Without irrigation the HYV is totally destroyed. The Indarasan variety is also more remunerative in the market, selling at Rs. 208 per quintal compared to Rs. 175 per quintal for Pant-4.

In Philippines on 29 May, 1986, the MASIPAC Centre (Farmers and Scientists for Agricultural Science Development Centre) was inaugurated in Jaen, Nueva Ecya. The centre's programme is to build an agricultural alternative which is not dependent on capital and external inputs as the Green Revolution was. Worldwide examples of successful alternative agriculture exist and are growing, even while they continue to be ignored by the dominant world-view of agriculture. And it is these initiatives that carry the seeds of a sustainable agriculture. Blindness to these alternatives is not a proof of their non-existence. It is merely a reflection of the blindness.

Biotechnology Development and Biodiversity Conservation

The central paradox posed by the Green Revolution and biotechnology development is that modern plant improvement has been based on the destruction of the biodiversity which it uses as raw material. The irony of plant and animal breeding is that it destroys the very building blocks on which the technology depends. When agricultural modernisation schemes introduce new and uniform crops into the farmers' fields, they push into extinction the diversity of local varieties. In the words of professor Garrison Wilkes of the University of Massachusetts, it is analogous to taking stones from a building's foundation to repair the roof. And as Brain Ford-Lloyd and Michael Jackson elaborate,

> Current international activities surrounding the genetic resources of plants aim to confront one paradoxical problem. This that scientists throughout the world are rightly engaged in developing better and higher yielding cultivars of crop plants to be used on increasingly larger scales. But this involves the replacement of the generally variable, lower yielding, locally adopted strains grown traditionally by the products of modern agriculture — the case of uniformity replacing diversity. It is here that we find the paradox, for these self-same plant breeders are dependent upon the availability of a pool of diverse genetic material for success in their work. They are themselves dependent upon that which they are unwittingly destroying.

The paradox arises from the foundational errors of assignment of value and utility, which then make the 'modern' varieties look inherently superior, whereas they are superior only in context of increased control over plant genetic resources and a restricted production of certain commodities for the market.

The challenge of the 1990s is based on our getting rid of false notions of obsolescence and productivity which legitimise the extinction of large parts of nature and society. The push for homogenisation and uniformity comes both from the transnational corporate sector, which has to create uniformity to control markets. It also comes from the nature of modern research systems which have grown in response to the market. Since most biotechnology research is dictated by TNCs, the sought out solutions must have a global and homogenous character. TNCs do not tend to work for small market riches, but aim at large market shares. In addition, researchers prefer tasks that can be simplified enough to be tackled systematically, and that produce stable and widely applicable outcomes. Diversity goes against the standardisation of scientific research.

There is, however, a prevalent misconception that biotechnology development will automatically lead to biodiversity conservation. The main problem with viewing biotech as a miracle solution to the biodiversity crisis is related to the fact that biotechnologies, are, in essence, technologies for the breeding of uniformity in plants and animals. Biotech corporations do talk of contribution to genetic diversity.

As John Duesing of Cuba Geigy states

> 'Patent Protection will serve to stimulate the development of competing and diverse genetic solutions with access to these diverse solutions ensured by free market forces at work in biotech ecology and seed industries.'

However, the 'diversity' of corporate strategies and the diversity of life-forms on this planet are not the same thing, and corporate competition can hardly be treated as a substitute for nature's evolution in the creation of genetic diversity.

Corporate strategies and products can lead to diversification of commodities, they cannot enrich nature's diversity. The confusion between commodity diversification and biodiversity conservation finds its parallel in raw-material diversification. Although breeders draw genetic materials from many places as raw material input, the same commodity that is sold back to farmers is characterised by uniformity. Uniformity and monopolistic seed supplies go hand in hand. When this monopolising control is achieved through the molecular mind, destruction of diversity becomes more accelerated.

As Jack Kloppenbur has warned

> 'Though the capacity to move genetic material between species is a means for introducing additional variations, it is also a means for engineering genetic uniformity across species.'

Production is thus driven into the direction of destruction of diversity, which swallows all biodiversity into its domain of colonisation. Production based on uniformity becomes the primary threat to biodiversity conservation, even though in the convoluted political economy of the market, it is cited as the reason for conservation. 'The exploitation of genetic adversity for crop improvement should be the ultimate objective of genetic resources exploration and conservation,' it is argued.

The arbitrary inequality created in the status of germplasm, creates an arbitrary separation between production and conservation. Some people's germplasm becomes a finished commodity, a 'product', other people's germplasm becomes mere 'raw' material for that product. The manufacture of the 'product' in corporate labs is counted as production. The reproduction of the 'raw' material by nature and Third World farmers is mere conservation. The 'value added' in one domain is built on the 'value robbed' in other domain. Biotechnology development thus translates into biodiversity erosion and poverty creation.

The main challenge to biodiversity conservation is the removal of reductionist blinkers which make more look less and less look more. The social construction of this deceptive 'growth and productivity' is achieved by :

(1) excluding crops and parts of crops as 'unwanted'

(2) creating a false hierarchy of resources and knowledge splitting diversity into dichotomy.

Not till diversity is made the logic of production can diversity be conserved. If production continues to be based on the logic of uniformity and homogenisation, uniformity will continue to displace diversity. 'Improvement' from the corporate viewpoint, or from the viewpoint of western agricultural research is often a loss for the Third World, especially the poor in the Third World. There is therefore no inevitability act against diversity. Uniformity as a pattern of production becomes inevitable only in a context of control and profitability.

All systems of sustainable agriculture whether of the past or the future work on the basis of the perennial principles of diversity and reciprocity. The two principles are not independent but interrelated. Diversity gives rise to the ecological space for give and take, for mutuality and reciprocity. Destruction of diversity is linked to the creation of monocultures. Sustainability and diversity are ecologically linked because diversity offers the multiplicity of interactions which can heal ecological disturbance to any part of the system. Nonsustainability and uniformity means that disturbance to one part is translated into a disturbance to all other parts. Instead of being contained, ecological destabilisation tends to be amplified. Closely linked to the issue of diversity and uniformity is the issue of productivity. Higher yields and higher production have been the main push for the introduction of uniformity and the logic of the assembly line. The imperative of growth generates the imperative for monocultures. Yet this growth is, in large measure, a socially constructed, value laden category. It exists as a 'fact' by excluding and erasing the fact of diversity and production through diversity. Sustainability, diversity and decentred self-organisation are therefore linked, as are unsustainability, uniformity and centralisation.

Diversity as a pattern of production, not merely of conservation, ensures pluralism and decentralisation. It prevents the dichotomising of biological systems into 'primitive' and 'advanced'. Like Gandhi challenged the false concepts of obsolescence and productivity in the production of textiles by his search for the spinning wheel, groups across the Third World are challenging the false concepts of obsolescence in agricultural production by searching for seeds used by farmers over centuries and making them the basis of a futuristic self-reliant and sustainable agriculture.

Patents, Intellectual Property and the Politics of Knowledge

Like the spinning wheel was rendered backward and obsolete by an earlier technological revolution, farmers' seeds are rendered incomplete and valueless by the process that makes corporate seeds the basis of wealth creation. The indigenous varieties or landraces, evolved through both natural and human selection, and produced and used by Third World farmers worldwide are called 'primitive cultivars'. Those varieties created by modern plant breeders in international research centres or by transnational seed corporations are called 'advanced' or 'elite'. The tacit hierarchy in words like 'primitive' and 'elite' becomes an explicit one in the process of conflict. Thus the North has always used Third World germplasm as a freely available resource and treated it as valueless. The advanced capitalist nations wish to retain free access to the developing world's storehouse of genetic diversity, while the South would like to have the proprietary varieties of the North's industry declared a similarly 'public' good. The North however, resists this democracy based on the logic of the market. Wiliams, Executive Secretary of IBPGR has argued that, 'It is not the original material which produces cash returns'.

A 1983 forum of Plant Breeding, sponsored by Pioneer Hi-Bred stated that,

> 'Some insist that germplasm is a resource belonging to the public, such improved varieties would be supplied to farmers in the source country at either or no cost. This overlooks the fact that 'raw' germplasm only becomes valuable after considerable investment of time and money, both in adapting exotic germplasm for use by applied plant breeders in incorporating the germplasm into varieties useful to farmers.'

The corporate perspective views as value only that which serves the market. However, all material processes also serve ecological needs and social needs, and these needs are undermined by the monopolising tendency of corporations.

The issue of patent protection for modified life-forms raises a number of unresolved political questions about ownership and control of genetic resources. The problem is that in manipulating life-forms you do not start from nothing, but from other life-forms which belong to other — may be through customary law. Secondly, genetic engineering and biotechnology does not create new genes, it merely relocates genes already existing in organisms. In making genes the object of value through the patent system, a dangerous shift takes place in the approach to genetic resources.

Most Third World countries view genetic resources a common heritage. In most countries animals and plants were excluded from the patent system until recently when the advent of biotechnologies changed concepts of ownership of life. With the new biotechnologies life can now be owned. The potential for gene manipulation reduces the organism to its genetic constituents. Centuries of innovation are totally disvalued to give monopoly rights on life-forms to those who manipulate genes with new technologies, placing their contribution over and above the intellectual contribution of generations of Third World farmers for over ten thousand years in the areas of contribution, breeding, domestication and development of plant and animal genetic resources.

As Pat Money has argued

> 'the argument that intellectual property is only recognisable when performed in laboratories with while lab coats is fundamentally a racist view of scientific development.'

Two biases are inherent in this argument. One, that the labour of Third World farmers has no value, while labour of Western scientists adds value. Secondly, that value is a measure only in the market. However, it is recognised that, 'the total genetic changed achieved by farmers over the millennia was far greater than that achieved by the last hundred or two years of more systematic science-based efforts'. Plant scientists are not the sole producers of utility in seed.

The utility of farmers' seeds has high social and ecological value, even if it has no market value attached to it. The limits of the market system in assigning value can hardly be a reason for denying value to farmers' seeds. It points more to the deficiency of the logic of the market than the status of the seed or the farmers intellect.

There is no epistemological justification for treating some germplasm as valueless and common and other germplasm as a valuable commodity and private property. This distinction is not based on the nature of the germplasm, but on the nature of political and economic power.

Putting value on the gene through patents makes biology stand on its head. Complex organisms which have evolved over millennia in nature, and through the contributions of Third World peasants, tribals and healers are reduced to their parts, and treated as mere inputs into genetic engineering. Patenting of gene thus leads to a devaluation of life-forms by reducing them to their constituents and allowing them to be repeatedly owned as private property. This reductions and fragmentation might be convenient for commercial concerns but it violates the integrity of life as well as the common property rights of Third World peoples. On these false notions of genetic resources and their ownership through intellectual property rights are based the 'biobattles' at FAO and the trade wars at GATT. Countries like US are using trade as a means of enforcing their patent laws and intellectual property rights on the sovereign nations of the Third World. US has accused countries of the Third World as engaging in 'unfair trading practice' if they fail to adopt US patent laws which allow monopoly rights in life-form. Yet it is the US which has engaged in unfair practices related to the use of Third World Genetic resources. It has freely taken the biological adversity of the Third World to spin millions of dollars of profits, none of which have been shared with Third World countries, the original owners of the germplasm. A wild tomato variety (Lycopresicon chomrelweskii) taken from Peru in 1962 has contributed $ 8 million a year to the American tomato processing industry by increasing the content of solùble solids. Yet none of these profits or benefits have been shared with Peru, the original source of the genetic material.

According to Prescott-allen, wild varieties contributed US $ 340 million per year between 1976 and 1980 to the US farm economy. The total contribution of wild germplasm to the American economy has been US $ 66 billion, which is more than the total international debt of Mexico and Philippines combined. This wild material is 'owned' by sovereign states and by local people.

Patents and intellectual property rights are at the centre of the protection of the right to profits. Humans rights are at the centre of the protection of the right to life, which it is threatened by the new biotechnologies, which are expanding the domain of and drive for capital accumulation, while introducing new risks and hazards for citizens.

The words 'freedom' and 'protection' have been robbed of their humane meaning and are being absorbed into the double-speak of corporate jargon. With double-speak are associated double standards, one for citizens and one for corporations, one for corporate responsibility and one for corporate profits.

The USA is the most sophisticated in the practice of double standards and the destruction of people's rights to health and safety in the Third World. On the one hand it aims at keeping regulation for safeguards restricted to its own geographical boundaries, while on the other hand it aims at destroying the Indian Patents Act of 1970 and replacing it with a strong US-style system of patent protection which is heavily biased in favour of the industrially developed countries.

The US government considers the transnationals' lack of patent protection as unfair trading practice. It does not consider the destruction of regulation for public safety and environmental protection as unethical and unfair for the citizens of the Third World. The USA wants to limit and localise laws for the protection of people and universalise laws for the protection of profit. The people of India want the reverse — a universalisation of the safety regulations protecting people's right to life and livelihoods and a localisation of laws relating to intellectual property and private profits.

All life is precious. It is equally precious to the rich and the poor, the white and the black, to men and women. Universalization of the protection of life is an ethical imperative. On the other hand, private property and private profits are culturally and socio-economically legitimised constructs holding only for some groups. They do not hold for all societies and all cultures. Laws for the protection of private property rights, especially as related to life-forms, cannot and should not be imposed globally. They need to be restrained.

Double standards also exist in the shift from private gain to social responsibility for environmental costs. When the patenting of life is issue, arguments from 'novelty' are used. Novelty requires that the subject matter of a patent be new, that it be the result of an inventive step, and not something existing in nature. On the other hand, when it comes to legislative safeguards, the argument shifts to 'similarity', to establishing that biotechnology products and genetically engineered organisms differ little from parent organisms.

To have one law for environmental responsibility and another for proprietary rights and profits is an expression of double standards. Double standards are ethically unjustified and illegitimate, especially when they deal with life itself. However, double standards are consistent with and necessary for the defence of private property rights. It is these double standards which allow the life the livelihoods of the people and the planet to be sacrificed for the protection of profits.

The resistance to such technological shifts requires that we widen the circle of control and decision-making about technology, by treating technology in its social and ecological context. By keeping human rights at the centre of discourse and debate on new technologies, we might be able to restrain the ultimate privatization of life itself.

During the first industrial revolution and its associated colonisation, Gandhi had transformed the 'primitive' spinning wheel into a living symbol of the struggle for India's freedom and self-determination. The 'primitive' seeds of Third World peasants could well become the symbols of the struggle for freedom and the protection of the Third World and its living resources.

9

Gender and Society in India

The Gender

WOMEN'S STUDIES are the academic response to the need to understand, analyse and remedy gender inequality and its various manifestations found in almost all societies. The goal of women's studies is to usher a gender equal social order and it is in this context that women's studies provide a critical analysis of the subordination, oppression and discrimination to which women have been subjected. Women's studies also refers to a body of literature that embodies concerns for gender equality and women's development. It tries to uncover the roots of gender based subordination, oppression and discrimination which go deep into history. Women's studies also aim at gaining an understanding of unequal power relations that exist in our society and create an environment for removal of these gender based inequalities. Studies on women are primarily concerned with questions relating to realities of women's lives in society and using the knowledge so generated to transform the social order. In this sense, women's studies is not simply a body of knowledge that focuses attention on women's needs, problems and perceptions but a critical instrument to empower women and men to question, protest and set gender inequalities right.

Women's studies is a discipline that has emerged out of gender concerns. Therefore, the major objectives of women's studies are :

(1) To draw attention to the consequences of "gender differentiation" on women's lives.

(2) To highlight the contribution of women in family, economy and society.

(3) To understand and analyse women's perceptions of their own lives and to enable them to take control over their lives.

(4) To identify the roots and structures of inequality which are responsible for the subordination of women and discrimination against them.

(5) To sensitize society about gender inequalities and the need to remove these and built an egalitarian society.

One of the major tasks of women's studies in the academic is to make women and issues of gender equality visible in the curriculum and to do this in a gender sensitive manner. Women's studies also aim at enriching the academic disciplines by integrating women's issues in a theoretical framework.

Though women's studies focus attention on women, all studies on women do not automatically qualify to be labelled women's studies. Women's studies need to develop a perspective which is feminist and which believes in analysing issues pertaining to women with an open mind. A feminist perspective is committed to obtaining an understanding of gender inequality, and looking at the world from a woman's viewpoint. Women's studies treat women as a category for analysis and promotes a multi disciplinary approach in order to incorporate women's experiences and understanding. Women's studies scholars have questioned the gender coloured assumptions of mainstream disciplines and argued that knowledge cannot be generated and interpreted by excluding half the humanity, *i.e.* women. According to the Programme of Action 1992 which is a follow up of the National Policy of Education 1986, women's studies is a critical input to promote better understanding of women's contribution to social processes, their struggles, aspirations and conceptual obstacles that make them invisible in many areas of scientific inquiry.

The initiative for launching a separate branch of studies related to women's issues and to use gender as a category for analysis from a feminist perspective generated in the United States of America. A large number of women entering institutes of higher education during the post war period became aware of the gender discrimination prevalent in various social institutions. This discrimination was specially evident in jobs, wages and unequal representation in scientific and technical courses. They felt the need to uncover the various facets and roots of this discrimination through empirical inquiry and later went on to theorize this discrimination. The feminist movement in England and other western countries also kindled the fire of search for answers to questions of gender related oppression and brought forth the need for a deeper analysis of questions of gender discrimination and oppression. Soon, women's studies became part of the university system in these countries.

Though many studies on women were carried out in India prior to 1975 women's studies as a subject with an identity of its own is of a more recent origin. Women's studies in India did not grow specifically out of the women's movement but it emerged because a few academicians in different disciplines felt the need to develop a forum for theoretical debates and analysis of gender issues. They were also interested in sensitizing the community to women's issues and committed to bringing about social justice and gender equality. It is very important to note that though women's studies in India did not grow out of the women's movement, the various issues brought up by the movement certainly gave an impetus to women's studies.

There were several factors that contributed to the growth of women's studies in India. The Report of the Committee on the Status of Women in India brought to light the prevalence of widespread gender discrimination of different social institutions. The declaration of the International Women's Year and the International Women's Decade drew increasing attention to gender related issues. The ICSSR (Indian Council for Social Science Research) Programme on women's studies, the establishment of the SNDT university's Research Centre for Women's studies, concerns over women's status and gender equality questions expressed by international agencies, the rise and growth of the feminist movement in India have all been factors responsible for the growing interest in women's studies. The various international conferences on women, the declaration of the SARC Decade of the Girl Child and the availability of funds from many government and voluntary organizations also gave an impetus to the growth and development of women's studies. The establishment of women's studies centres and cells in universities and colleges across the country was a step which was successful in drawing the attention of the academic community and the public at large towards the need and significance of women's studies. Teaching, research, training and extension have all been integrated into the scheme of women's studies.

Women's studies covers a wide spectrum of gender issues and interested women's studies specialists have been trying to find a place for the subject in main stream social science disciplines. Concepts such as "role", "status", "patriarch", "violence" are now being examined from a new perspective. Issues such as women's status, health, violence against women, impact of religious ideologies have been highlighted by women's studies. Though women's studies research in this country has been subject to the influence of western writings on women's issues, a large number of academic initiative have been inspired by issues of regional relevance. The need to develop "grass-roots" theorization about questions affecting women in India has been fully realized. Yet another development that is heartening to note is the firm footing established by women's studies in the process of planning and framing policies for women's development. Because of the growing realization about the role of women in country's development (one may say that this realization is itself a result of earlier studies on women) more and more donor agencies are commissioning studies on "gender impact and gender implications" of programmes, policies and projects. Findings of research studies have also been used in advocacy, gender sensitization programmes and women's development initiatives.

There are mainly four types of institutions promoting women's studies in India. They are :

1. Centres of Women's Studies supported by the University Grants Commission.
2. Independent and autonomous centres engaged in research and action. These institutions are either supported by state grants, financial support by state grants, financial support received from international aid agencies or other autonomous institutions.
3. Women's rights organizations conducting action research that provide inputs into campaigns or actions.
4. Autonomous, quasi-government or government supported research organizations that promote research on women conducted by individual research scholars and faculty.

The pedagogic logic of introducing women's studies in the university system is that academic discipline must be imbibed with the gender perspective. As of now most academic disciplines tell only half the truth because the experiences of women and realities that characterize the lives of women who form half the world have be excluded from knowledge. "University" means the whole, the total. Hence if universities must live up to their highest goal, *i.e.*, the search for the whole truth, women's studies must become an integral part of the university system.

The Women's Studies Models

While there is no dispute about the fact that women's studies should find its way into the university curricula, an important factor that must be borne in mind relates to the model which needs to be adopted while teaching and learning women's studies. The two important models which can be considered while introducing women's studies in the university system are :

1. The Integrationist Women's Studies Model
2. The Autonomous Women's Studies Model

The Integrationist Women's Studies Model believes in introducing women's studies into the man stream disciplines. In other words, it aims to spread the perspectives of women's studies into different disciplines. The integrationist model aims to bring about change by penetrating main stream disciplines. Adding the gender dimension to teaching units wherever there is a scope or adding new chapters on women's issues are among the strategies adopted by the integrationists.

The autonomous Women's Studies Model on the other hand, is different. The viewpoint of this model is that women's studies neither shares the assumptions of dominant cultures nor does it find the compartmentalization of knowledge adequate to pursue the questions which it raises. The autonomous women's studies model believes in an "in depth" approach as well as in introducing feminist insights into the process of knowledge acquisition and knowledge transmission. The autonomous women's studies model does not simply believe in introducing a course of women's studies or a few topics on women. The basic purpose of this model is to ensure that women's studies should alter the fundamental nature of knowledge itself by shifting to a frame of reference in which the experiences, needs and interests of different groups of women are recognized and honoured.

Questions have often been raised on the ideal model that needs to be adopted while trying to introduce women's studies into the university system. If our goals include sensitization of the university system, introduction of women's perspectives into the curriculum and also to spread our net wide, the integrationist model is perhaps the best. But if we intend to develop a theoretical base, initiate an ongoing dialogue with activists and feminist scholars, to serve the women's movement as a powerful resource base and also to analyse the impact of the women's movement on society and the state, the autonomous women's studies model may serve our purpose more effectively.

Women's studies is both discourse and an agenda for action. It is very crucial that a proper perspective must be adopted while teaching women's studies courses. Students and teachers of women's studies must be motivated to act against those forces that create and perpetuate to raise questions about the different forms of gender biases operating both overtly and covertly in various social institutions. It is difficult to achieve these targets by adopting conventional methods of teaching such as for example, offering a mass of information. The following are some of the methods that are likely to yield the most effective results in a women's studies classroom :

1. Utilizing learner's experiences, observations etc., as basis to generate discussion and dialogue.
2. Making use of newspaper clippings, posters, charts and other material rather than relying on textbooks only.
3. Using oral histories, biographies and folk materials.
4. Adoption of innovative teaching methods such as assignments based on field work, seminars and extension activities.
5. Involvement women's development programmes being organized by the state or voluntary sector.

Women's studies also emphasize alternate methodologies of research to capture the experiences of women. It questions the emphasis that main stream disciplines lay on such concepts as "objectivity" and "value neutrality". Women's studies scholars however, argue that no research is "value neutral" or "totally objective". Objectivity according to them is only a perspective and the main stream disciplines look at reality from a male perspective. If women's studies perspectives have to be brought to the forefront feminist methodology advocates an approach which raises basic questions about existing social structures that are oppressive. In fact feminist scholars have raised fundamental questions about the nature of knowledge itself.

With the initiative taken by the University Grants Commission, women's studies has found a place in academic programmes at different levels of higher education. Women's Studies Cells have been established in many universities and colleges. The centres are primarily committed to promoting teaching, research and extension activities in the area of women's studies. The target groups include students, teachers, administrators, professionals and people in different walks of public life. Women's studies centres also act as catalysts of change in the academic community and are striving to spread knowledge about gender related issues by canvassing for their inclusion in the curricula of different disciplines. Networking with voluntary groups and state agencies is also on the agenda of women's studies centres. In the long run centres of women's studies and cells in colleges are expected to change the present attitudes and values in society regarding women's roles, potential and responsibilities.

A review of the functioning of women's studies centres in different Indian universities shows that not all these institutions have been able to achieve all the targets laid down by the guidelines of the University Grants Commission. At times working within the constraints of a university bureaucracy might throw up certain challenges. Also, the rigid social structures might make goal achievement at rather hard task.

If women's studies centres have to function effectively a certain amount of flexibility must be built into the university system. Right from introduction of courses to appointment of teachers and research staff, universities must take into account the unique nature of women's studies. The subject which is essentially multi disciplinary in nature and perspective must be handled by scholars and activists drawn from different discipline backgrounds. All these issues are not however, mutually exclusive. When administrators and faculty become gender sensitive all the problems might be resolved to a logical end.

Yet another heartening development in the field of women's studies is the organization of a series of seminars, workshops, conferences and training programmes on different themes in women's studies. There has also been virtual boom in the number of writings on women. However, it has to be accepted that not all these writings are created from a gender perspective. In such a case the material may either become writing "on" women "of" women instead of "women's studies" material.

Because of the availability of funding and the interest that has been sustained in women's issues a large number of researchers have been working and writing on women. But unless a feminist and gender sensitive perspective is adopted these writings will not carry much weight. It is very important that teachers, researchers, students and others who are speaking and writing about women need to get oriented to the special characteristics and needs of women's studies. It is not just enough to undertake descriptive or exploratory research only, theory building must also form an essential component of women's studies writing.

Despite all the skepticism and apprehensions that are being raised about the academic responses to women's issues it can be said that women's studies in India have found a firm footing both within and outside the university system. It has made a significant contribution in highlighting gender issues in the country, besides of course influencing policy perspectives and state interventions.

Women's studies is only a phase in creating a body of knowledge that includes women's experiences and realities of women's lives. Once this knowledge building and dissemination gain momentum and a situation is so created when individuals and institutions have been sensitized to respond to gender issues, there might perhaps be a stage when there will no longer be a need for a separate discipline of women's studies! One has to wait and watch.

FEMINISM AND THE INDIGENOUS KNOWLEDGE SYSTEM INDIA : AN EXPLORATION

Exploration of Knowledge System

The observation that the position of women is subordinated to that of men in both Europe and India is in most cases correct. However, the observed inequality of women in the two subcontinents has a fundamentally different reason. In this paper the researcher purposes to look at feminism in India from the vantage point of the Indian Indigenous Knowledge Systems. This implies an interdisciplinary approach which draws on insights given by indologists, historians, sociologists and anthropologists.

The reference to Europe is given for two reasons. First, inequality usually entails hierarchy. The concepts of hierarchy in Europe and India are essentially different. Secondly, the feminist movement which originated in Europe has spread to India during the past two decades. This movement gained substantial support in India on the basis of perceived similarities of practices, but ignored the concepts lying behind them.

An attempt is made to analyse feminism in India by uncovering the concepts behind practices of inequality. It does not attempt a comparative study of the position of women in Europe and India as such a project needs at least a volume length of attention.

A few basic concepts of the Indian civilization are described followed by the theoretical conclusions which are illustrated with a few ethnographic examples. In the next section the concept of hierarchy in Europe and India is discussed with reference to inequality. The comparative approach with reference to perceptions of society and the person, and the structure of the Indian society and how it is visible at the level of the household are presented. With reference to the three Indian tradition — the Scriptural Tradition, the Traditional Practices and the Modern State — the threats to and the problems of the feminist movement in India are also described.

Root Paradigm

The unity of the Indian civilization cannot be formulated in terms of the political and social economic system. For India the unity of the culture is to be sought in its value system defined as a recognition of the transcendent order. Louis Dumont was the first to emphasize this. The transcendent order is the order where all worldly distinctions such as the one between life and death are superseded. The order generates an idiom in which the relationships or connections of the world are justified or rejected.

Typical Indian is the formulation of the opposition pure : impure. The ultimate aim is to protect the pure (that which is connected with life) from the impure (that which is connected with death). The Indian civilization recognizes two possibilities to guarantee the continuity of life (purity) against death (the impure).

Based on an analysis of both the Vedic and classic texts, has given an interpretation which is paraphrased here. The first possibility consists of cyclic exchange of the pure (life) and the impure (death). In ancient India this was dramatized in agnostic feasts in which the opposition is represented by the host and guest. The host presents gifts to the guest who by the same token burdens the guest with death. *Concretely, the death of the animal sacrificed served to the guest.* Through this act the host gains life. Obviously this hospitality calls for a reciprocity.

The ancient texts show that this cyclic exchange became obsessive and a new direction was developed. Thus a second possibility evolved, namely, an axial break through the cyclic reciprocity through absolution of the pure, (life), liberalized from the cyclic exchange. The Indian civilization has opted for a value system which is based on the severance of reciprocity and interdependence. Consequently, absolute purity was placed outside the world. Many individuals could strive for this position by turning their back to the world. The world-renouncer (*sannyasi*) has withdrawn from the various circle of interdependence, and most literally, transcends the social world. The renouncers as individuals unite within themselves oppositions and through this act, so as to speak, they themselves become the all (universe).

The Indian value system is based on this form of transcendence. The transcendent order can be reached by one who leaves the interdependent order of the social world.

The religious order compasses the worldly order. He denies the breach between the two orders, the world is not encompassed but in principle disconnected from the transcendent sphere.

Dharma

Contradiction is also central to the *dharma*. On the one hand there is the prescription to sacrifice animals and the serving of non-vegetarian feasts to the guests. On the other hand there is the prescription of absolute vegetarianism.

Significantly, both the spheres coexist where both recognize the transcendent order as the highest principle.

The unity of the Indian civilization is a value system which acknowledges the transcendent order. The values form a point of reference for real life. But the two spheres coincide. Society has to legitimate itself in an idiom that contradicts it "the inner conflict of (Indian) tradition".

Varna : Kinship Exogamy

An important term of the legitimating idiom is *varna*. This means that a particularistic society based on interdependence has to legitimize itself in terms of a theory that purposes substantial units with attributes, without relationships and without interaction.

The historical development of the *varna* theory was analysed. Originally there was a system which classified the entire world, including its flora and fauna, into four principles analogous to the four cardinal points and four seasons. From this system evolved the ideal of four groups connected through a circulating connubium. Later these groups break up and become four strictly separated categories (*varna*).

However, the *varna* theory breaks up society in the same way as the Vedic ritual. According to Hessterman "It does not stop at dividing society into four strictly separate blocks but goes a long way in breaking down the internal cohesion of each *varna* too. This becomes clear when we look at the *rules pertaining to marriage*. One should, of course, marry within one's *varna*, but the rules about forbidden degrees of relationship (*sapinda* relatives) are such that they exclude the otherwise normal — even normative — practice of marrying within the circle of known relatives (such as one's mother's brother's daughter). If strictly adhered to as, of course, it hardly ever is or can be — the prohibition would prevent the formation and maintenance over the generations of a web of marriage exchange. The exclusion of the *sapinda* relatives would cause the affinal network to crumble with each new generation, leaving the single patriline isolated. The intention clearly is to atomise society.

Jati : Kinship Endogamy

In the world, there are thousands of actually functionary groups to which one belongs by birth. These groups are the *jatis*. The *jatis* are interdependent, and collaborate with each other. It is these connections that the *varna* theory purposes to eliminate by disconnecting status from power. This leads to Brahman being acknowledged as the highest and purest because of absence of power and his autonomy. Ideally he does not have provisions for the next day. A problem for field workers is that informants give statements about their actual situation interim of an idiom which is in principle contrasted to it.

In other words, the traditional practices who *jatis* based on kinship endogamy and commensality while the *varna* theory proposes kinship exogamy according to the *sapinda* rule.

Two Models or Respectability

The absolute break between the transcendent and immanent orders leaves the world with only the option to strive for emancipation. Where the Brahman represents the ideal type of emancipation, the king represents the world of interdependence and exchange. The Brahman option keeps the social world at a distance of withdraws from its interdependence. The Kshatriya option is one of participation in social interdependence. In Hessterman's interpretation, as we have seen on the Goddesses of Tirunelvely District.

Not only historically but also from the Vedic and classical texts it becomes clear that the importance of the Goddess has been changing. It was the great Ideologist professor Kuper who drew attention to this : "A peculiar treat of the Vedic pantheon is the absence of formidable female figures such as Athena or Hera with Homer or Durga or Kali in later Hinduism."

The power of the Mysore Wodeyar was vindicated by the Brahman, but this authorized power could only be made operational by the involvement of the Goddess Chamundi.

The separation of the transcendent order of perfection and non-violence from the immanent order of the social world implies in the world an ideal of disintegration for the person who wishes to reach the ultimate liberation and who should thus not be attached to the globe. The central ideology leads logically to disconnections between all element which make up society. In other words disconnection of elements, discontinuity of values and disintegration of units in society is its principle.

The modern government as a successor to the king, so clearly in the field of patronage for the artisans, is seen engaged in a similar act as the king. Obviously, the power of government is legitimized by the elections. The voter in the election booths is the modern *avatar* of the Brahman who vindicates the power of the modern "king" or government of the Goddess, *e.g.*, through worshipping her in her manifestation of a river or the *darshan of a guru* to get its policies implemented.

In the old dispensation the triangle Brahmin-ing-goddess can be seen at both the superlocal and local levels of government whereby the king could be a *maharaja, raja* or *noble* man of a lower order. In institutions, are seen patronizing either a goddess, a Maruti temple or a deity to a *guru* is in line with the increased popularity of *bhakti* cults. The essence here is the concept of neutrality for both the chosen male deities or the *guru* are in principle "above the parties or without a party" as the expression has it.

Indian ideology is thus marked on the one hand by a static transcendent order of completeness, protection and non-violence placed outside the world. We may visualize this as the brahmanical involution of all into a single point. Its complementary opposition is the mundane order of a trinary structure which in the political domain is represented by the Brahman, king and Goddess or the voter, the government and the guru.

The "axial break through" which split the turbulent order of the world from the static transcendent order calls for ingenious ways in the world, particularly for the brahman, to cope with the dilemma. Detachment from the world is the ideal of all. In religious terms the *atman* and the *brahman* have to unite in the transcendent order which is only possible when both have no attachment in the world.

For the classical brahman two solutions were found : the four *ashramas* on the individual level and the king's gift for the brahman which is given to the deity on the collective level. To the present-day the renouncer can reenter into relation with the world where he can enjoy unequalled prestige through his *impartiality*.

The root paradigm of a perfect and static, all distinctions superseding, objective transcendent order and the dynamic, imperfect, if not conflictious and interdependent order of the world, calls for a trinary structure in the world. The logic is simple. The complementary opposition between the exclusive category and the inclusive category is based on the former's need for livelihood (the fruits of "power") and the latter's need for "authority," (the vindication of "power"). The exclusiveness of the one category makes the structure at once unworkable and a third element needed. For the king it was the Goddess; for the government it is the Goddess or the *guru* in the political domain. In the social domain of sub-castes it is again the Goddess or the *guru*. In the domestic domain it appears as the independent or impartial order of the *puja* room, the *purohita* or visits to the temple or *matha* as the neutral element and the householder (power) and his wife (to make the power operational) as the first and second element of the structure.

The Modern State and Feminism

In the foregoing sections, the term Modern State was used in the context of the concept of the person. The Modern State is

India's third tradition beside the Scriptural Tradition and the Traditional Practices. The Modern State in India is a little over 200 years old, but it suffered from two contextual constraints. First, it began in a colonial form and only after 1947 it became sovereign. Secondly, it never replaced the other Indian traditions, but was juxtaposed to them.

The modern, industrial democratic state functions on the fiction that society comprises of a collection of individuals. Its unity is mediated by abstract, impersonal rules and principles. All individuals are equal before the law. Inequality, however, slopped in where something went wrong with "horizontal" pattern of distribution of resources.

The Modern State as we know it today evolved from the philosophy the enlightenment in Europe with its ideology of modernity and the ideal of equal rights. In the cause of the various industrial revolutions, the first feminist movements occurred in mid 19th century, especially in Germany. The feminist movements were means to correct the pattern of horizontal distribution as regards gender too. Feminism is thus a result of the Modern State itself. This is particularly clear regarding one of the major roles of the women's movements in Europe, namely, the acquisition of full citizenship.

Today feminism in Europe finds itself between modernity and postmodernity, while in India it finds itself between the Modern State and Traditional Practices. Women in India, if feminists, have to emancipate not only from the failures of "horizontal" distribution of the Modern State, but also from the personal bonds of "vertical" hierarchical interdependence.

Even if the utopia of perfect horizontal distribution were achieved, Indian feminists would still find themselves in a society where two, perhaps three distinct concepts of the person prevail, namely, the first tradition of the individual outside society with an integrated concept of multiple self; the second tradition of individuals with separate multiple self; and the third tradition of individuals inside society with a concept of the unitary person?

The concept of the unitary person, as Mary Douglas demonstrated is linked with the European perception of society divided into separate judicial, political, economical, social, cultural and religious domains. In this perception the cause-effect chain takes place with each single domain of reference.

The European feminists have not yet achieved full citizenship in practice. This a tragic situation, for the process of the "death of the citizen" has already been set in motion. The consumer democracy in which the citizen has been transforment into a consumer, is rapidly replacing the emancipation of women by the emancipation of the sign.

Thus, the degree of success of feminism in India depends on the degree of success of the Modern State in terms of real "horizontal" pattern of distribution. If, however, feminism is directly implanted in the traditional practices it risks reinforcing the individual's colonism at the cost of relationship and dialogue thus weakening both the women's movement and the modern state.

The feminist movement in India has to keep in mind the trinary structure of society, the prevailing concepts of the person and the perceptions of logical domains of reference these are :

Indigenous knowledge not only refers to the knowledge of indigenous people, but also to that of any other defined community. Quite often Indigenous Knowledge is local, but it need not to be traditional as knowledge is always in the making.

The term *Indigenous Knowledge System* (IKS) delineates a cognitive structure in which theories and perceptions of Nature and Culture are conceptualised. It thus includes definitions, classifications and concepts of the physical, natural, social and economical.

- *Indigenous Technical Knowledge* is seen as one of the expressions of the IKS. It refers to the practices in which underlying concepts have to be found in the Indigenous Knowledge Systems as a whole.

- The essence of Indian civilization is thus the opposition and separation of two spheres. Throughout history and today new attempts have been made to bridge the irreconcilable opposition. The deity of *bhalur* encompasses both the transcendent and immanent spheres. Here, the devotee remains in the world, but disowns the result of his actions. He dedicates his action results to the deity through which act he hopes to unite with the deity.
- In modern idiom, friendship, hospitality, accountability and responsibility are forms of relationship. They are thus expressions of attachment in different domains of society. There are two contrasting perceptions of these forms : they are either operationalized as part of a maximalization of interactions or made incidental as part of a strategy of minimalised interactions.
- There are thus two options for man's emancipation from the social world in order to reach total detachment; the inclusive model of maximized transactions and the exclusive model of minimalized transactions.
- In contemporary European culture, the idea of selfhood is a conceptual space deliberately kept open. In this culture questions of identity are not easily settled. This given the individual the option to define him (her) self his or her own identity in a process of egoistic or altruistic creativity, either intellectually or empirically, in the social world. In Indian culture the self is an articulated concept, contextualised, and conventionally defined. In such a situation one may expect less room for generating creative action and achievement.
- Modern science is axiomatic in its conception of Nature as distinct from Culture, hence Culture can study Nature. It is also axiomatic in its belief in cause-effect thinking.

> Western perspective regards Nature as "a linear phenomenon in which what happens in a given place and time is determined exclusively by what has occurred at nearby places immediately beforehand". In other words, in western thinking, the cause-effect chain takes place within single logical domain of reference.

These axioms made it possible to distribute Nature and Culture into different fields of study to the extent of losing sight of the whole. The holistic approach by contrast allows to consider the structural relationships of various such reference fields of categories from the vantage point of a topology.

It has to be borne in mind that this is significantly different from much of the non-western sciences, in which the holistic view assumes Nature to be intrinsically non-linear, so that "non-local influences predominate and interact with one another to form a complicated whole."

As early as 1967, the Rudolphs were the first to recognize the modernity of tradition. According to them : "Brahmanic law as Britons understood it bore some resemblance to the law of modern legal professionals : it was available in written texts; although diverse, its cosmopolitanism gave it an air of generality and uniformity that parochial, customary law lacked; and it was interpreted and applied by a class of legal specialists. Its subsequent role as a vehicle of modernisation is related to these attributes." Perhaps the appeal to feminism in India has to be explained in the existence of a "natural bedding" for feminism in India's first tradition. Although feminist usually proclaim that man and woman are equal but different, this comes close to the principle of identification of opposites which we find in the Scriptural Tradition. Here, identification is a technique to preclude relationship. Feminism and the "modernity of tradition" seems thus a matter of urgent anthropology.

Feminism as an emancipation of women from a male oriented 'horizontal' pattern of distribution of power is gradually overshadowed by the emancipation of the sign and its equation of "real" contents that gave it weight or form as representative equivalent. As Baudrillard puts it : "The emancipation of the sign : released from any 'archaic' obligation it might have had to designate something, the sign is at last free for a structural or combinatory play that succeeds the previous role of determinate equivalence."

The Empowerment of Women Hinduism

Religion provides answers to ultimate questions such as the meaning of life and death and explanations for injustice, inequality and unfairness in life. It also determines a sense of personal worth by providing evaluations of people and determining their status in society. Rituals that punctuate social life and the individual life cycle help people to develop an inner conviction regarding the legitimacy of positions accorded to them in society. Thus religious symbolism provides connections between the sacred and secular aspects of life. Religion is also an important source of inspiration for many people since it holds up ideals to strive for in life. These statements hold true in general whether people are overtly religious or not because religion consistently influences the popular belief systems and the taken-for-granted realities of social life. In addition, the institutional structures in any given society are informed by the religious tenets thereby providing an aura of legitimacy to the existing order of things. Thus, as Geertz points out, religion provides moods and motivations for people to organize their lives.

For women, religion is a mixed blessing. In general, women need religion as much as men do to make sense out of life and find inspiration to carry on. But most of the known world religions at the present time are patriarchal. Therefore, the male principle is given primacy, men are defined as reflections of the image of god, conceptualized as more worthy and therefore, considered as more entitled to be in control. Women are made to feel as the "other", less worthy, and the one with the inferior body, mind and soul, and therefore, deserving to be controlled and dominated. Religious rituals and symbolism confirm and legitimize this state of affairs as just, proper and in keeping with the natural order of things.

Most religions include in their religious tenets at least some women-friendly strands. More often than not these aspects are obscured and ignored because, by and large, men have been in charge of interpreting religion and presenting it to the public. Consequently, just as in other institutional contexts in modern societies, men have established themselves as the dominant group and have been directing the course of events.

To bring about gender equality women have to actively participate in all institutional arenas, including religion. For women to become active participants they have to be empowered. Empowerment means that women develop an inner strength and confidence in themselves and come to believe they are worthy people. It also means that they become aware of the significance of their contributions to society, and believe in their right to make choices in life and influence the direction of social change.

Such empowerment requires access to material resources as well as gaining religious legitimacy for gender equality. It is one of the arguments that by exclusively focusing on material aspects of social change, women cannot be motivated to participate in bringing about their own emancipation. There is a constant and dialectical relationship between ideological and material forces. Ideologies are the form and material forces are the content. For example, industrialization can provide women access to economic resources thereby enabling them to question male domination. On the other hand, in a rigid ideological environment, gender ideology of male superiority can determine the nature of participation of men and women in the process of industrialization.

Under such circumstances industrialization takes place within the context of gender ideology of male dominance and female subordination. This means men will enjoy the benefits of industrialization while women continue to play their traditional role. To circumvent such an outcome as, new ideologies have to be forged and made popular through reinterpretation of tradition and history. In this context woman friendly strands of religion need to be highlighted and made popular to promote the ideology of gender equality. Old ideologies are not projected and new ones accepted simply because they are more rational, just, or good. They are accepted only when there is a popular acceptance of the new and rejection of the old. The efforts of intellectual and more leadership are crucial at this juncture. They have to highlight the woman-friendly aspects of religion to gain religious legitimacy for gender equality. When the ideology becomes popular, conditions are conducive for the empowerment of women.

Religious Ideology on Women's Lives

Hinduism, just as most other religions, accords women a secondary status by promoting *pativratya*, which literally means husband worship. This ideology stipulates that women must find self-fulfilment in this life and salvation hereafter through unswerving devotion and service to their husbands. For a wife, her husband is the person god. She has no separate identity but is an integral part of her husband. This belief system is considered consistent with the natural order of things and therefore, legitimate. A woman, it is believed, is owner of a body that is susceptible to ritual pollution, and a mind that is impulsive, whereas a man's body is ritually pure and his mind steadfast. Women provide soil to nurture the seed of life provided by men and personify undirected energy which is dangerous unless controlled and directed by consciousness personified by men. Therefore, for an orderly fruitful life that is in keeping with the natural order of things, men should be in control. This ideology historically has informed the institutional structures and social practices in Indian society.

Even though the intensity of commitment to this ideology has varied over time and across regions, it has provided the framework and inspiration to women's lives historically as well as in contemporary society. The lives of women and girls in Indian society can be understood and appreciated only when we place them in the context of this ideological framework.

Predicament of the Girl Child

This ideology has impacted on the treatment of girl children. Even though there are regional variations in the degree of devaluation of girl children in general it cuts across classes and castes, as well as the rural-urban continuum. Parents justify their preference for sons on several grounds, one of them being that sons are of symbolic significance. They carry the family name and give oblations to parents which ensures safe spiritual journey. On the other hand, girls belong to someone else. Statements like, "Bringing up a daughter is like watering a neighbour's tree" are made. Many women literally glowed with pride when they talked about their sons. On the other hand, many mothers said they would rather not give birth to a daughter, who would be a sinner just like themselves.

Parents look upon daughters as a drain on family resources because of the expenses incurred not only in bringing them up, but also on their marriage, including dowry. Daughters are considered a burden and an inconvenience in day-to-day life because their virginity must be protected. There is a very strong belief that a girl must be a virgin until marriage.

These convictions have given rise to many practices which are detrimental not only to the health and well-being of the girl child, but also, in some circumstance, to her very survival. Sex ratio has been consistently in favour of males over several decades and has become more so in recent years. Several studies demonstrate that family resources are unequally distributed among children, with girls suffering from chronic malnutrition. The infant mortality rate is higher for girls than boys. Parents take care of the health of sons much better than daughters. Investment in girls' education trails behind that of sons. Incidence of foeticide and infanticide is much greater for girls. However, daughters are expected to work harder and start working as early as they can. Mothers, over-burdened with work, depend on daughters to ease their own drudgery, sometimes even at the expense of the daughter's future and her well-being.

Subordinate Position

The behaviour of women can be understood only when we place it in the context of women's subordinate position in the family. The dominant family pattern is patriarchal, patrilineal and patrilocal. Until she gives birth to a son, the daughter-in-law's position in the family is marginal. Husbands have absolute control over wives and consider them inexhaustible resources they can draw upon. Violence and threats of violence make them submit to such control. In general, wives are economically dependent on husbands since they are usually denied inheritance rights. Women's primary identity, sanctioned by religion, is that of a wife. No other meaningful, morally equivalent lifestyle is available for them. Lone women are easy prey to sexual predators since they are thought of as loose women without male protectors.

In general, women are socialized to be dependent (Dhruvarajan). Consequently most women develop a negative self-image and a sense of low self worth. Prejudice and discrimination are part of the daily life experience of women and girls. Religious rituals and symbolism systematically erode their self-confidence by making them believe they are less worthy than their male counterparts. A girl's body is believed to be susceptible to rituals pollution and she is assumed to have uncontrollable impulses. To protect her purity and preserve the family honour, she is made to believe she should be under the control of elders and does not deserve freedom of movement like her brothers. Going through such experiences, women learn to despise themselves and despise women in general.

Women, conceptualized primarily as wives and mothers, are embedded in the household despite the fact that one-third of households are headed by women. In addition to being exclusively responsible for housework and childcare, women have always made contributions are considered mere extensions of their homemaking role and not recognized as important. Women's work in general is devalued. Housework and childcare are not even considered because women are considered dependent, despite their contributions, men are given better opportunities in the labour market. Even when women find employment, they are paid less than men for the same or similar jobs.

Gender equally has been enshrined in the Constitution of independent India, but women's lives are circumscribed by custom and religion. This is because the constitution has also enshrined freedom of religion. Laws are distinguished as civil and personal laws, the latter being governed by religion and custom. Personal laws include those relating to marriage, divorce, property inheritance, custody of children — in general all those that govern family behaviour. In the political process, gender equality is not considered an end in itself, but only one of the goals which is often superseded by other goals such as promoting freedom of religion. The result that the family acts as a state-within-a-state as far as the lives of women are concerned. Religion legitimises these circumstances and the state adopts a hands-off policy.

Development Efforts in India

The expectation that the status of women will improve when development is well underway has not been realized. Even though many middle class women in urban areas have benefited to some extent from development efforts, the consistent finding of many studies has been that women's status in general is systematically deteriorating. This is particularly true for women in rural areas, where the majority of the population resides. To date, gender issues have not been recognized as political issues, and awareness of gender inequality is lacking. Only in the sixth plan, for the first time, a separate section has been added which addresses the issues of concern for women. In the seventh plan, attitudinal change in society regarding involvement of women in development is recognized as important to address women's issues. The need for voluntary efforts by non-governmental agencies to achieve this goal is stressed. As it is evident, analysis of the cause of women's predicament does not go far enough because, these development efforts have been guided by thinkers who adhere to Women in Development Model (WID).

WID thinkers argue that gender inequality is largely due to traditional values and male ignorance. They believe this can be corrected through legislative reform, attitudinal changes and intervention projects designed to proved for basic needs through income-generating work. Women in this context are treated as passive recipients of development initiatives rather than active participants. Family/household is considered as the unit of analysis and women and conceptualized primarily as wives and mothers. This has been detrimental to women, particularly in poorer households which deny them recognition as producers. As a result, women are denied equal access to employment, credit, technology, education and training. Empirical evidence shows that women are being edged out of the labour market in agriculture, trade and commerce, as well as cottage industries, or are pushed down to the bottom of the labour hierarchy. Some other contributing factors for women's exploitation are sex segregation of labour, taboos on freedom of movement and participation in certain jobs. In additional, women are predominantly in the unorganized informal sector of the economy. Considering the household as the unit of analysis and assuming that if the household benefits women will also benefit, has resulted in targeting households for welfare programmes. Many studies demonstrate however, that males and females do not equally benefit if households benefit. Men and boys get a disproportionate share of the benefits even in basic necessities such as food, health, clothing and also in education.

Another result of centuries of exploitation is that women themselves accept their role as wives and mothers and not as workers. This attitude make women vulnerable to exploitation. In addition, those women who are overburdened with housework and childcare tend to express a feeling that they would rather give up paid work if their husbands can support them. Such an outlook often leads to judgements by employers that women are not motivated and committed workers.

Empowerment of Women

One important insight gained from analysis of the development process is that without the active participation of women in the formulation and implementation of policies and practices related to development, gender equality cannot come about. Women must be considered agents of development rather than targets of development agencies and planners. Women must define their own needs and goals as well as strategies. A prerequisite for women's participation in development process is empowerment.

Historically, several reformers argued that gender inequality and caste inequality are integrally related. The goal of resistance movements in this framework was to bring down the hegemony of Brahmins. As recent events indicate, the struggles of lower castes to shed Brahmanic stronghold of power have been successful to a large extent, even though still have some way to go. The lower castes are in a numerical majority. The spread of consciousness among these people has facilitated gaining of political power in a democracy where size of the electorate is important. But the status of women has remained unchanged, because in general the struggles in lower castes are headed by men. Lower-caste men achieve economic betterment their behaviour becomes Sanskritised. This means, the lower-caste women, who had a slight advantage over upper-caste women in gender relations because of Dravidian cultural influence, are deprived of that advantage as lower-caste men take on the behavioural patterns of upper-caste men.

As India became urbanized and industrialized, the ideology of gender equality has emerged among middle and upper middle class women who benefited from this process. They are questioning the legitimacy of the ideology of *pativratya* and are attempting to replace it with the ideology of gender equality. One can identify broadly two different seats of strategies followed by feminist intellectuals and moral leaders in this endeavour to empower women. The first set of strategies has been to focus attention primarily on structural transformation. The second view adopts a holistic approach where structural changes and changes in ideologies are paid attention to.

Empowerment through Structural Transformation

Jawaharlal Nehru, the first prime minister of India and one of the founding fathers of the nation, was a firm believer in this strategy. He argued that dependents are never free. Under his leadership, gender equality became enshrined in the Constitution when India became a republic in the '50s. Since then constant efforts have been made to bring about legal changes to reinforce political/legal legitimacy for gender equality. Efforts have been made to give women economic, political and educational entitlements at par with men. There is a growing realization that more needs to be done in these areas to make a difference in the lives of women who are confined within patriarchal families. Nevertheless the argument is that families do operate in the context of larger society. Therefore, both explicit and implicit messages can be sent to family members to revise the standards of behaviour.

It is argued the both positive and negative sanctions can be applied to send message to family members that girls are valued members of society. Making welfare programmes gender sensitive and making special provisions for girls to have access to the basic necessities of life sends the message to parents that girls are considered worthy of special attention in the society at large. Passing laws that prohibit murder, abuse and neglect of girls will send a message that girls are not expendable. Passing laws against sexual predators and enforcing them diligently will make the streets safer for girls and this makes the job of bringing up girls. All of these actions are of immediate importance, because of the kinds of messages they send to parents.

Bringing about a uniform civil code applicable to both men and women is considered most important in this context. It is the personal laws governed by religion and custom that continue to keep women in a subordinate position. Removing the dichotomy between civil and personal laws would go a long way towards responding to women's concerns. The laws in the personal domain concern marriage, inheritance, divorce, adoption and custody of children — in essence, they determine women's status in the family. A uniform civil code will make gender equality a living reality for women's lives, thereby circumventing the patriarchal stranglehold. This conceptualizing provides a positive framework for making opportunities equally available in the context of development initiatives. It also provides conditions conducive for positively evaluating women's contributions to the domestic economy and questioning the sex stereotyping of labour. The policies and programmes are more likely to be gender sensitive because, in this context, gender issues could become political issues. Women can be considered as having equal entitlement to credit, upgrading of skills and access to new technology.

A consistent opinion among feminists who argue along these lines is that structural changes necessarily led to ideological changes. Once women become educated, they will become economically self-reliant which leads to their lives becoming more secularized. Under such conditions religion ceases to exert much influence. But what is actually happening is that development policies are being informed by religious ideology. This has determined the direction of social change in such a way that modernization is taking place within the ideological framework. As has been shown, the consequence is that women have been incorporated into this process without changing the nature of gender relations. Religion still has a tremendous hold on women's lives. It is a mistake to underestimate the significance of a religion which has provided guidelines for women's lives for hundreds of years.

Empowerment through a Holistic Approach

There is a growing realization among feminists that focusing exclusively on economy, education and politics will not solve the problems women are facing. While it is true that women cannot be liberated without economic independence, it is recognized that mere earning activity without awareness of self worth is futile.

The emerging view is that development efforts should be multipronged. They should focus on structural changes as well as changes in ideologies/belief systems. The conviction is that empowerment of women is possible only under such conditions. There are several feminist efforts in this direction. The arguments feminists are making to obtain religious as well as legal legitimacy for bringing about autonomy and self-reliance for women. Struggle must continue at both ends because they are integrally related. Feminists argue for continuing the struggles on economic/political fronts and for changing the assumptions regarding gender relationships informed by religious ideology. These arguments are made drawing upon several historical precedents.

The feminists are not completely rejecting all the ideological practices, but are analysing the belief systems and social practices by identifying their historical roots and religious legitimization. The general strategy has been to reinterpret history and religion and articulate them within the framework of gender equality and suggest social practices that promote this ideology. This is precisely the kind of process Gramsci identifies as transformational. The new ideologies attempt to replace the old ones by going through a process of reinterpretation and rearticulation of history and promoting social practices that are consistent with the new world-view. The feminist focus has been on reinterpretation of religion in such a way that it retains spiritual essence without misogyny.

Historically, social reformers have made efforts to questions various social practices that limit women's lives in the name of religion. Attempts have always been to separate the basic essence of Hinduism and social customs that emerged under various social circumstances. Interpretations differed depending upon time and place as well as the personal interest of these reformers. One can identify three different types of such efforts. The most common type has been to accept women's basic identity as that of wife and mother. The firm conviction is that a woman's self-fulfilment and salvation lives in discharging these duties while maintaining dignity and self-respect. The focus is then to ensure that conditions are conducive for women to discharge these duties. Mahatma Gandhi is a typical example of such reformers, along with many others. Gandhi maintained that there should be equality in gender relations. He exhorted men to be cognizant of their responsibilities as husbands and fathers, and discharge their duties diligently. He reminded women that they have every right to hold the men responsible for their obligations. He rejected the stipulation that women should be docile even when men behaved irresponsibly and callously. In keeping with this spirit, Gandhi advocated different curricula for men and women — men in the educational system to prepare themselves for the labour force, women for service to the family and community.

This is a departure from the past. Women were confined to their prescribed roles because they were deemed as undeserving of any other role but one of subservience to their husbands. Gandhiji, on the other hand, advocated gender equality within the home. He rejected the notion of pollutability of the female body. Instead he was full of admiration for the caregiving role women so competently provided historically. He tried to instill in women a sense of pride for being women and for being able to provide indispensable services as wives and mothers. He advocated a sex-typed division of labour but promoted gender equality. He gave sanctity to women's bodies and marvelled at their will power. He considered women morally superior because they lead a life of selfless service and withstood so much suffering. Many Indian women revere the Gandhian tradition because he made them feel worthy. He instilled pride and dignity in them by valuing the contributions they made to their families and helped them to develop positive body- and self-image. This is, in a very important sense, an empowering influence.

Nevertheless, Gandhi was not in favour of economic self-reliance for women. He argues that women have a moral responsibility to uphold the family. He believed that their exposure to the world outside would corrupt them. He considered women to be morally superior but this dubious honour came with a heavy burden. Women were always expected to be selfless, self-sacrificing and spend their lives serving the interest of others, particularly their families. The ideal he held up to women was that of Sita, the epic heroine who spent her lifetime serving the interest of her husband, epic hero Rama. He favoured women becoming social workers to rid society of social evils, particularly women who rejected marriage and motherhood. Gandhi's position has the potential for the empowerment of women to the extent that he made women felt that the kind of work they do within the home is important and they have an option to reject marriage and motherhood in favour of selfless service to humanity in general.

The restrictions on women achieving economic self-reliance and the sex-typing of their labour have a confining effect of women's lives. Gandhi's prescriptions were similar to that of lawgivers of ancient times, for example Manu, but Gandhi different in the way he interpreted women's roles. While ancient lawgivers in general cast aspersions on women's character, worth and ability, Gandhi evaluated them positively. He also opened the door for feminist reformers to reinterpret ancient scriptures and depart from them. This he did by explicitly stating that he found it difficult to abide by the infallibility of scriptures while they denied freedom to so many women and constrained their lives. He argued further that to swim in ancient tradition is good but to sink in it is suicide.

Another argument is that men's and women's roles and relationship change according to time and place. Culture is not something that remains static and rigid but evolves as circumstances change. One example is caste relations in contemporary India, where hierarchy is de-emphasized as disenfranchised caste are claiming their rightful position. The caste system, at present, in interpreted as not being an integral part of Hinduism but rather something that evolved over time to adopt to social circumstances. In the same vein the orthodoxy of men in day-to-day affairs has been relaxed in modernized urban India. Men have changed their dress, hairstyle, and daily religious rituals as they have adopted to the changing work situations. In the same way, it is argued that women also can change as they become part of modern India.

The status of women has been different in certain periods of Indian history. She demostrates how women's status was much better during Vedic times but systematically deteriorated afterwards. Women during the Vedas had more autonomy in their lives. They had a right to education, could choose their mates and the marriage age was older than it is now, women had more freedom of movement and some control over their personal belongings. She gives many examples of women who were well versed in the Vedas and Upanishads. Wives chastising husbands, and wives carrying on conversations as equals with husbands were common place. The term "*Dampathi*", meaning couple, signified equal status to husbands and wives in household affairs. Even though the family system was still patriarchal, patrilineal, women's rights were not completely transgressed.

There are also examples of some saints who defied tradition and rejected marriage and motherhood. Instead of worshipping husbands as gods, they worshipped a god considering him as husband, thereby gaining autonomy in their lives. At that time, it was the appropriate way for them to defy religious customs. In the same way, women in modern India can make choices they think are appropriate in their lives by defying customs and traditions.

Another view is historians were selective in presenting images of women to suit their own political agenda. Various epic heroines of the past are portrayed differently in different texts depending upon the context in which the text was written. In more recent years, the docile, shy and obedient images of epic heroines are presented for emulation to women, even though many other portrayals of the same characters as confident, articulate and assertive were in fact available.

The interpretation of the nature, countenance, characters and powers of goddesses has been altered within the patriarchal framework drawing upon evidence provided by oral tradition, archaeology and non-scriptural religious practices in different parts of the country, they demonstrate how there was a struggle historically between native Dravidian conceptions of divinity and that of invading Aryan conceptions. Eventually the natives were conquered and subjugated and Aryan hegemony was established. But the Dravidian matrilineal traditions could not be completely obliterated. Instead, the divine principle of Dravidians, where the goddesses had a powerful presence, was incorporated into Aryan patriarchal religion. The goddesses were stripped of autonomous existence and integrated into the male gods in a secondary position. No longer were goddesses worshipped as autonomous divine principles but an appendages to the Aryan gods, they were given the status of docile wives. Lone goddesses were conceptualized as impulsive and unruly, thereby invoking fear of disorder and chaos.

At present, in many regions of India, particularly in the south, all villages have a patron goddess who is believed to supervise the affairs of the village and protect the villagers from internal and external enemies. She also makes sure that villagers are law-abiding citizens. She is conceptualized as wise and strong. She is capable of being perturbing and caring, as well as fierce and strong according to the demands of the situation. When villagers worship this goddess it is to pray for her nurture and care as well as protection. There is an implicit faith in her ability to do the needful. These goddesses are generally patronized by the lower caste people, and they are looked down upon by the dominant culture.

Retrieving Dravidian goddesses with all their glory, beneficence, power and autonomy will significantly alter the position of women. The goddess represents nothing less than the spiritual essence present in every women. Consequently, invoking the goddess in every women will be liberating and uplifting. Women, instead of feeling devalued, deprived and relegated to the margins, can feel worthy, pure and entitled to all the privileges and responsibilities life has to offer. Thus it can be an important source of inner strength and confidence for women to strive for goals they set for themselves.

Various rituals and symbolism evident in non-scriptural traditions of goddess worship have become corrupted by patriarchal interpretations. Even though these rituals provide context for women to develop a sense of community, in fact the meanings of these rituals have been distorted to such an extent that they only serve to perpetuate patriarchal hegemony. Instead of celebrating womanhood and the joys and excitement of their life experience as women, (menstruation, pregnancy, and childbirth to name a few) women end up praying for sons and long lives for husbands and atoning for the sin of being born women. These interpretations are more stringent among Brahmins, while Vokkaligas, a Sudra Subcaste have more woman-friendly interpretations. For example, rituals celebrating a girl's first menstruation express joy for the awakening of her sexuality rather than dwell on the ritual pollution of her body as the Brahmins do. A sense of positive affirmation of womanhood is stressed rather than a negative resignation to one's destiny of subordination because of pollutability of the female body.

Concluding Remarks

Possibilities exist for positive reinterpretation of religious beliefs and practices by drawing upon the lost/devalued/ suppressed Dravidian traditions of India. This will have a positive impact on redesigning women's status and bring about gender equality. In fact, in the state Kerala where Dravidian traditions area not completely lost, women far relatively better on all indices of gender equality.

There is room for optimism regarding the possibility of establishing religious legitimacy for equality. In fact, in one of studies on Hindu women who are first-generation immigrants to Canada, there is a firm conviction that misogyny is not an integral part of Hinduism — therefore, gender equality is possible to achieve. Most of these women have rejected the notion of pollutability of the female body. They are very proud of the religious heritage that acknowledge the capabilities of women to achieve, the reverence accorded to women as mothers, and the inspiration provided by the presence of female divinity. In other words, these women are selectively borrowing from the religious tradition to affirm integrity and pride in their womanhood.

Trends of Change in Scheduled Caste Women in an Urban Setting

It is a well recognized fact that women do not constitute a homogeneous category. The socio-economic and cultural context in which women are placed must be given due consideration in analysing issues pertaining to them. In the existing literature on development two contradictory revelations have been made. First, the guarantee given by the state that there shall be no gender discrimination in determining access to development opportunities. Second, the fact that there is sufficient evidence to show that development has perpetuated the existing social and economic inequalities and that it often marginalizes and exploits the already oppressed groups.

Development is not an inherently equalizing process. If has two basic components, *viz.*, the material-emphasizing the increase in productivity and non-material-aiming at improving the quality of life. The first is inevitably the result of technological advancement, and the second is the result of social welfare measure. But there is severe inequality in access to utilization of development opportunities. Social justice remains an elusive goal until basic socio-economic inequalities are removed. This ethics of redistributed justice needs to be introduced through specific interventions. Development through planned social change is aimed exactly at such specific interventions that restrain or remove conditions of disparities.

The Constitution of India has made certain special provisions for the welfare and development of the scheduled castes and tribes, in view of the peculiar nature and extent of the social and economic disabilities suffered by these groups for centuries.

In pursuance of these Constitutional safeguards, the Planning Commission and the Government of India have been issuing guidelines right from the introduction of the First Five Year Plan to the state governments to see that benefits flowing to people under the general sector go to the weaker sections in general and Scheduled Castes and Scheduled Tribes in particular, realizing that the supplementary grants given to the welfare departments are meant only for taking up certain special programmes for the speedy progress of these people. This was specially intended to reduce the disparities between the Scheduled Castes and the rest of the population in different spheres of development. It has however, been found that this discrimination continues to exist in newer forms and in newer dimensions. This discrimination assumes serious proportions in the case of scheduled caste women who are engaged in occupations considered unclean.

The Balmikis rank at the bottom of the Hindu social structure. They are the lowest among the former untouchable. As Ibbetson writes : "Socially they are the lowest of the low, even lower than the vagrant Sansi and the Gipsy and as a rule can hardly be said to stand even at the foot of the social ladder. Issacks also comments on this aspect as follows : "Night soil has traditionally been the task of untouchables at the bottom of even the untouchables scale. This kind of scavenger is known as Bhangi and Bhangis are a people apart even among people apart."

Issues related to women have been attracting some attention in recent years, especially in the context of development and change. It is now widely recognized that our development programmes have not succeeded to the extent desired. Some sections of our population like the Scheduled Castes and Tribes and their women in particular have been either neglected or denied their due place in society.

The present paper focuses attention on the scheduled caste women of Uttar Pradesh. One of the major concerns in studying their socio-economic conditions is to raise certain pertinent questions keeping in mind their present condition. These questions primarily relate to the extent and nature of change achieved by the development programmes. It is hoped that the findings of the study will throw light on the problems of development of women in general, and backward groups, in particular.

In urban areas of Uttar Pradesh, women sweepers and washer women along with their men folk are still carrying on their traditional occupations mostly because of the low status assigned to these castes are moving out to their traditional jobs. But women have far fewer chances of mobility. It is, therefore, interesting to have a close look at their social conditions.

Methodology

Moradabad is an important industrial centre of Uttar Pradesh. It is also known for its large scale exports and employment opportunities. It occupies an important place in the socio-economic and political life of the state. As per the census of 1991, the population of Moradabad is 4,29,214. It is estimated that there are 34,100 persons who are scavengers, Balmikis and Lalbegis (a sub caste of Balmiki).

The study was conducted in two phases. In the first phase a census of the city's 5000 families of scavengers was carried out to collect basic information. In the second phase a sample of 100 families was interviewed with the help of an interview schedule. This was supplemented by group discussions and talks with leaders of their group.

Early Studies

Brief references to the living conditions of scheduled castes in India are available in the accounts of travellers as well as in government reports published from the beginning of the 19th Century. In Bihar, some references are available in the journals of Mamilton Buchanan in the first quarter of the 19th century. More detailed accounts are available in Huntor's (1868) *Statistical Annals of Bengal*. Later, considerable amount of information about various major and minor scheduled caste groups was available from the volumes on castes and tribes in different parts of India.

It is only in the beginning of the 20th Century that more detailed studies of scheduled castes in the form of monographs began to be available. The studies were sponsored by the Young Men's Christian Association of India and they formed part of a series called "Religious life of India."

An informative account of the reform movements among the scheduled castes is available. The report of the Commissioner for Scheduled Castes and Tribes says that the scheduled castes were not allowed to follow the customs and traditions of upper castes. This is a view also that trends of social change were perceptable in the Chamars of Satnami sect. It is also one view that status of Balmiki women has definitely improved on account of change in the occupational status of their men folk.

A number of studies have opined that changes have taken place in the status of scheduled castes. It is, however, true that change has not affected all the scheduled caste groups in a similar manner. It is a universal truth that among the marginalized groups women are more marginalized than men. So scheduled caste women have borne the brunt of oppression to the greatest possible extent for centuries. They were also virtually invisible in studies on women. It is only in recent years that empirical studies on scheduled caste women are being taken up by scholars.

A Socio-Economic Profile of the Respondents

The sweepers of Uttar Pradesh are known by different names such as Bhangis and Balmikis. They are responsible for maintaining the cleanliness of the urban civic system and continue to perform duties of a *Jajmani* nature in specific mobility are open to a caste which hitherto occupied a lower position in the caste hierarchy, it is mostly the men who garner these opportunities and women continue to suffer from age old deprivations. Commenting on the role of female bhangis in a

Village in the Karimpur district of Uttar Pradesh and the 1930s, the Wisers felt that "they had to perform the most unpleasant task in the village". That was the removal of excreta from the floor of high caste houses.

The study reported that each sweeper woman used to make daily visits to the house of her conservative employers, where women were kept under strict *purdah* so much so that they did not even go out to the fields for defecation. In each house a woman used to slink into the privy beside the courtyard or on the roof, keeping herself out of everybody's sight. The sweeper gathered the excreta from the earthen flow into the basket and carried it along with the refuse of other households to the fields.

During their second visit to Karimpur William Wisers found that a number of Balmikis were moving to the cities in search of jobs. The flush toilet system which was found in urban areas had made the traditional jobs of Balmikis less defiling. When the authors left Karimpur in 1930, males had started moving out of scavenging jobs. Some Bhangi men had become night watchmen and messengers for their jajmans while their wives, mothers and widowed sisters stayed back home to retain their jajmans. This trend is visible in the case of women sweepers of Moradabad too. Women tend to remain scavengers while their menfolk move out into jobs of a less defiling nature. Many of the educated sweepers are found in government jobs, banks and railway service. Women till today are private sweepers and some of them are also working in Moradabad Municipal Corporation while the other women are working as private sweepers in newly built colonies and residential areas. None of these Balmiki women seemed to have a hope of moving out of the traditional caste based occupation.

In Moradabad, the balmiki caste population is sprinkled over the whole city in 10 Busties (localities) such as Sambhal Phatak, Katghar, Delhi Gate, Indira Chauk, Bangla Gaon, Baradari, Kisrol, Nagphani and Lal Bagh. It was found during the course of field work that it is not unusual for many castes to cohabit the same locality without any apparent signs of tension. However, this is not to imply that caste distinctions have disappeared. Poverty has merely given priority to expediency over notions of purity and pollution. The areas where these sweepers live do not have central municipal lighting along the lanes. A few residents have taken illegal connections to their rooms from the street lights. There are a few latrines constructed by Sulabh Shouchalaya Organization and are put to use by the sweepers. About 50 per cent of the residents have their own water taps, while others use the municipal taps. Most of the families keep livestock like pigs and chicken.

A majority of the respondents in our sample were above 26 years of age, and were married when they were between 11 and 16 years of age.

Marriage outside the group is prohibited. They are strictly endogamous. Earlier, Brahmans did not officiate at the marriage of sweepers, but now the Arya Samajists and Brahmin priests not only fix the time and date of marriage but also officiate at the marriage rituals, at least in the houses of well-to-do Balmikis. During this period, however, they do not accept water or other edible items.

Dowry is still in vogue among the sweepers. In the case of child marriage, the bride is kept in her father's place till she attains puberty. Before she is sent to the family of her husband, a second nuptial called *gauna* takes place.

Monogamy is the prevailing form of marriage although they do not object to polygamy. Only a few have more than one wife. Both husband and wife have the right of divorce.

Alcoholism is very common among men. It often results in wife boring. While the men folk play cards, watch movies, or listen to radio their women have hardly any time to seek relaxation. By and large, all their time is spent in drudgery — either at home or at work. Time spent on jobs, housework and commuting leaves women with little time for relaxation. The respondents reported that they had no time to think of any leisure. Chatting with friends in the colony was the only form of relaxation.

Among the scavengers unemployment is rare. In the sample, majority of the families had more than one earning member.

Nearly three-fourths claim that their monthly family income ranged between Rs. 500 and Rs. 1,500. Only the wives of clerks and other corporation sweepers said that they were able to save. Incomes earned by women provided the family with the extra economic support essential for survival. However, the extent of indebtedness among the respondents seemed to be rather high. To meet out other obligations, more than two-thirds of the respondents borrowed and the amount ranged from Rs. 500 or less to Rs. 3,000. Most of these loans were taken to meet daily expenses. The rest of the respondents also borrowed in order to meet expenses incurred on rituals associated with marriages or deaths. Besides running the family women sweepers were constantly entangled in a process of debt repayment. Generations of them have worked to meet day-to-day needs and work seems to be the order of their life.

The wages which they earn reflect the economic condition in which sweeper women are placed. Payment for those working in private homes is very low. For their services, they are paid only Rs. 5 per house per month, and in the colonies and in the outskirts of the city, Rs. 25 per house per month. The extent of severe exploitation is evident from the fact that for a work, which a person from no other caste would do, these women are paid less than 17 paise a day. An appalling reality indeed. The dual standards so inherent in our wage structure are perhaps at their highest here. While for certain groups there is constant revision in pay scales, persons who perform the most condemned of all jobs are paid such low amounts. It is sad reflection on the values of a society which places a heavy premium on purity and cleanliness and those that help to preserve his cleanliness are treated with such conditions.

Not all sweepers have similar work experiences. Those who are in private employment clean latrines and take away household garbage to the refuse dump. But this is possible only in the case of development colonies where each house has the facility of flush latrine. The physical structure of these homes built by Avas Vikas Parishad and Moradabad Development Authority is such that sweeper women came into contact with items of everyday use. The bathing area and commode are usually situated on one room. While cleaning the toilet women sweepers are allowed to touch buckets, soaps and other articles used by the family. But, where the latrines are in the Indian style and are separated from the bathing place by a wall, there are strict taboos on the movements of these women. They are not allowed anywhere near the kitchen. In the old city, many of the homes still have service latrines where women sweepers have to clean the night soil too.

It is striking to note that in spite of this exploitation the Balmikis have not shown a readiness to accept change. The Government of Uttar Pradesh launched a scheme known as "*Swachchakar Vimukti Yojna*" to relieve scavengers from the burden of carrying night soil. Under this scheme an amount of Rs. 20,000 was given as loan to a scavenger to start a new occupation. Out of this amount fifty per cent was sanctioned as grant. The Moradabad Administrative Authority conveyed the information that the target set for this district was 300 beneficiaries but in spite of their best efforts only 67 persons could be given loan and the rest of the money was refunded to the state government. The Health Department and the city Municipal Corporation also informed us that scavengers were not coming forward to take the benefits and were not willing to leave their ancestral occupation and come out of the jajmani system.

From the data collected, it is inferred that the Balmikis of Moradabad still depend upon the jajmani system. The city has been divided into different blocks for the purpose of sweeping and removing refuse and certain number of sweeper families are in charge of each block. Each family has been servicing a certain number of houses (jajmans) for several years by now and this responsibility is handed down from one generation to the next. The jajmans compensate the sweepers for their work through periodical payment both in cash and kind and throughout the year. The sweepers also receive benefits, such as free food, clothes, raw materials, utensils, etc. The jajmani right of property passes from father to son.

There is marked difference between the parental generation and the present lot. One important future is that more Balmiki children are in primary schools now as compared to their parents' generation. However, more number of sons than daughters are in school. There is also a higher rate of dropout among daughters. The Balmikis, however, feel that there is nothing unfair about taking girls out of school because it is felt that under conditions of extreme poverty, daughters should help the family by looking after younger children while the mother contributes to the family income by working. In spite of the tree schooling facility for scheduled caste children, most of the respondents complain of the high costs of the educational materials.

The Balmiki women are very pessimistic about the chances of their daughters achieving occupational or social mobility through education. They have definite views about the future of their children. They hope that sons would move into non-traditional jobs, while most girls would combine jobs as jamadar with home making. It was obvious that slum dwellers did not consider education very important for their daughters. Even then it is heartening to note that literary rate of the second generation is much higher than that of the parents.

Religious beliefs and practices of the Balmikis are deeply rooted in amorphous convictions of philosophical Hinduism, animistic ideas, superstitions, beliefs and the cult of the mysterious world full of spirits who are both malevolent and benevolent. *Boots* (female ghosts), *Churails* (female ghosts) may seize both males and females and cause death to them.

The institution of *satsang* is a popular and socially significant characteristic of the scavenger's life. Of such sects only the Natha Panth, the Kabir Panth, the Dattatrey Panth, the Rama Nandi Panth are popular among them. Part of the religious ideology of the Naval sect has recently been fused with the social and political aspirations of the scavengers in their annual celebration of the birthday of the Saint Valmiki. They also worship Hindu gods. A majority of the women say that it is during religious festivals such as Shivaratri, Janmashtmi, Ramanavami and Deshera that they visit temple.

Political Consciousness

Scavengers are allegedly becoming more militant now, but are yet to achieve success in bringing about a change in the wage structure in the less affluent parts of the city. Women are so busy with their jobs and household chores that the question of taking time off to organize themselves does not arise. They are not ready to support the workers who agitate for better pay.

In traditional India mass illiteracy, conservation, geographical distances, extreme localism and a fairly rigid social structure cut off the great majority of the people from effective participation in political life of the country. In fact, the level of literacy is an indicator to assess the voting power of the scheduled castes *vis-à-vis* the voting power of the upper castes. While scheduled caste men have also not been able to attain the level of education as prevalent among the upper strata, the deprivations experienced by women are much more intense and are bound to affect their chances of political participation.

A majority of the respondents cast their votes but their voting behaviour is conditioned. Their vote is almost a preordained and a calculated one. Proclamations of equality of opportunity remain meaningless for them.

Development programmes and Five Year Plans have not touched the weakest sections of the society. Even within the backward regions the economically and socially weaker sections were kept outside the circumference of the development schemes. Benefits of planning did not percolate to the bottom.

Some Trends of Social Change

It is to be noted that till now, only a few attempts have been made to understand the nature of changes that are taking place among the scheduled castes of Uttar Pradesh. These changes touch some of the important aspects of the life of the Balmiki too.

In terms of occupational mobility scavenger women still pursue their traditional demeaning occupation despite special provisions for free education and reservation in employment. Urbanization has provided a scope for horizontal mobility. For instance, the sweepers have taken to truck-driving, gardening, factory work or securing jobs in class III and class IV cadres in the government. However, vertical mobility is seen only where the Balmikis have been able to receive higher education.

Some Balmiki men have been able to enter government services, professions and have become political elite. Balmiki women, however, have not been able to attain any occupational mobility. They have not been able to take advantage of the fruits of industrialization and urbanization. Professional and white collar jobs or small business are areas which are still closed to them. Even the existing opportunities for pursuing higher education in the form of scholarship and other incentives are not made use of by Balmiki women.

One sees an increase in the worship of Hindu Pantheon of gods and goddesses. All the Hindu festivals are celebrated. However, not all religious practices of upper castes are accepted. One change that is specially meaningful to women is the increase in the number of monogamous marriage and nuclear families.

Future Options

Systematic and organized efforts to empower the scheduled castes were made by the government only after independence specially in the light of the Constitutional provisions. But, it is by and large true that the scheduled castes in general and Balmikis in particular have not received many benefits. This is especially true of Balmiki women. They need serious attention from social workers and women activitists.

One of the main reasons for their continued low status is the low level of their literacy. Though during the last few decades there has been some progress in the educational attainment of men, the educational status of Balmiki women is still low. Majority of the Balmiki children are not sent to schools for various reasons such as economic handicaps, domestic problems, inadequacy of governmental assistance, etc. People in charge of schools should evince a special interest and devotion to promote the education of these children. It is not just a question of extending the facilities to them once. There should be a continuous follow up and monitoring. This work should be carried on with a missionary zeal. If the Balmiki women are to be empowered in the true sense of the term, schools with flexible timings and flexible calendars should be opened in large numbers. Many girls/women who are forced to work for a livelihood can attend these schools and gain access to knowledge.

10

Status of India's Health and Healing

Drought and Nutrition

MALNUTRITION IS a grave manifestation of drought, if not its only consequence, in 1987, India experienced a drought of great severity and magnitude. Yet again, the dependence of the country on the vagaries of nature was underscored. The paucity of rainfall adversely affected agriculture, but the impact on food availability of the macro level was minimal due to sufficient food stocks. The country as a whole used the buffers to absorb the shock inflicted by the drought. However, the poor do not have the luxury of such shock absorbers and in times of shortages, they are the most vulnerable.

The impact of drought on the nutritional status of India's widely stratified society cannot be explained simplistically. As the primary effect of drought is on agriculture, its worst victims in terms of nutrition are rural landless labourers and marginal and small farmers. As their diets are deficient in important nutrients (carbohydrates, vitamins and minerals) under normal circumstances, drought imposes additional stress on them. Even among this section, women and children are at greater risk due to a variety of socio-economic and cultural factors.

Water scarcity and crop failure are the main features of drought, resulting in a deficit of food, fodder and drinking water. The problem is compounded by the lack of employment for the landless and subsistence farmers, emigration of cattle, increasing indebtedness and distress sales of land and possessions. The scale and magnitude of these conditions, however, are directly dependent on the severity of drought and the destitution it causes among the people, in the ultimate analysis, it is a question of survival.

A notable feature of the 1987 drought was the near absence of starvation among the worst affected. The National Nutrition Monitoring Bureau conducted a study on the frequency distribution of the households by energy intake in the states of Gujarat, Orissa, Andhra Pradesh, Tamil Nadu and Karnataka. It showed that not one household in Gujarat or Andhra Pradesh was subsisting on a 'starvation diet' or consumed less than 500 K cal per capital per day.

With availability and access to the staple food having improved of the majority of the people, average energy intakes tended to approximate the level of 2,000 K cal (seen during non-drought period), except in Tamil Nadu (1,670 K cal). This was an improvement on the level of calories intake reported during earlier drought — 1,100 to 1,400 K cal.

However, if not substantially in terms of quantity (energy content), drought adversely affects the nutritive intake of its victims (vitamins, minerals and even proteins to some extent). The NNNB study of the 1987 drought found that under both during drought and non-drought conditions, most food items except stable cereal and millets are consumed much below the recommended dietary allowance (RDA). During the drought, consumption levels of almost all over clinical nutritional deficiency signs showed a definite increase. The signs of protein energy malnutrition (PEM), vitamin a deficiency and anaemia, especially among children and women showed an increasing trend. This has serious implications for the general health of the community.

The apparently 'better' situation observed in 1987 seems to reflect the efficient management strategy adopted : foodgrain distribution system, provision of relief works and implementation of feeding and other welfare programmes. Any effort aimed at ameliorating the nutritional status of those affected by drought has to be a comprehensive package which makes available both foodgrains, through an efficient distribution channel, and wages, employment opportunities, drinking water, nutrient supplements, water and livestock management systems and medical and health care.

Poverty and Malnutrition

In the words of M. Adiseshiah :

We are fighting each other over the precise number of the poor living with us. The numbers will vary with the norms used — calories, calorie/protein, calorie/cultural, health/housing, clothing or PQLI — and percentage would move a few points either way depending on the methodology used. But these definitional...problems do not change the stark fact.

The stark fact is the alarming scale of poverty in India, with the number of people below the poverty line exceeding the total population of the Soviet Union. They not only lack the resources to meet their minimum calorie requirements, but live in miserable environment conditions with no access to protect drinking water and sanitation facilities, thus putting them at risk to infection and disease.

Their poverty is further enhanced by prolific and unplanned childbearing. India's crude birth rate is 33.3 per 1,000 population (RGI 1981). At any given time then, there will be approximately 100 million pregnant and lactating women, 170 million preschool children (under 6 years) and 250 million school-going children (6 to 15 years). Furthermore, this will have grave consequences on the already vicious cycle of low birth weight female infants → malnourished adolescent → malnourished pregnant and lactating mother → low birth weight infant.

If India is not deficient in foodgrains today, the same will not be true by the turn of the century. While the average growth rate over the past five years has been 2.2 per cent, national foodgrain output had been a mere 1.5 per cent. Unless immediate steps are taken to check population growth, it will have deleterious consequences on the already grave problems of poverty and will be a major deterrent to the improved nutritional status of our population.

Socio-Cultural Factors and Malnutrition

Social and cultural factors influence the food consumption patterns of our population, which in turn have a significant impact on nutritional status.

The bulk of the Indian diet, unlike the Western diet, consists primarily of any one cereal : rice, wheat, maize, jowar or bajra. Of these rice accounts for 43 per cent of total cereal production, followed by wheat (33 per cent). As much as 60 to 80 per cent of our food is derived from any one of these cereals. Such an imbalanced dietary intake poses a nutritional risk for three reasons :

1. Should the crop of any one cereal fail, it would lead to a major crisis unless prompt action could be taken by the government to make up the deficit.
2. Any inherent defect in a particular cereal which forms the staple diet could result in serious nutritional disorders. For instance, pellagra occurs where maize or jowar are consumed in large quantities; beriberi in areas where polished rice is the staple food; lathyrism where the pulse lathyrus sativus (kesari dal) forms the bulk of peoples diets.
3. It has been found, however, that the selection of food items in the Indian diet is determined as much by economic constraints as traditional and tenacious food habits. A conscious effort to educate the people about the advantages or other foods could help overcome some of these problems.

Several other factors also impinge upon the nutritional status of an individual. These include : breast-feeding practices; weaning practices (timing, duration, quantity and type of weaning foods); intra-familial food distribution (male *vs.* female); child-feeding practices (who feeds the child — mother, siblings, others); occupational status of the mother and nature of occupation (distance from home); nuclear or extended family; decision-making within family, and food taboos.

While all these factors might not apply to all communities at all times, they highlight the fact the given the marginal status of households with regard to food availability, any one of these factors can determine whether a child will be well-nourished or malnourished and to what degree. An important factor that is assumed to have a significant impact on nutritional status is maternal education. Although no direct association has thus far been established, four possible relationships have been suggested and merit further study :

- *The two are more associates* : there being no cause and effect relationship.
- *Household economic effects* : better education → better marriage → better income.
- *Intra-household effects* : better education → better nutrition and health related knowledge → better weaning and feeding practices → better care during sickness → better spacing of children → higher age at marriage → personal hygiene → utilization of available resources and services.
- Historically, the incidence of nutritional disorders was perhaps negligible as long as people were able to eat well. Nutritional disorders emerged as public health problems once man began to exploit man — through slavery, feudalism capitalistic relations of production, unequal terms of international trade, etc. These exploitative relations led to the disruption of the ecological balance, which in turn compelled people to live in the most degrading ecological settings.

Nutrition science chained its pedigree from chemistry, biochemistry, physiology and clinical medical science. This cross-fertilisation triggered off a series of scientific breakthroughs : nutritional elements were identified, balanced diets established, the complex pathways in the metabolism of proteins worked out, and various forms of primary nutritional disorders identified as outcomes of specific deficiencies. In time, nutrition education, food processing and animal nutrition became additional components of the science of nutrition. Undoubtedly these advancements made a major contribution to the body of knowledge. However, with the increasing scientific content in this body of knowledge, the focus of studies moved further away from the problems of humans in their ecological settings. Instead, biochemical laboratories and animal houses became the venues for the study of human nutrition.

There are those, like D. Banerji, who argue that this shift in emphasis was not unintentional. Such research was promoted by market interests because nutrition became fertile ground for the rapid promotion of the food and drugs industries. The symptoms were emphasised while the root cause was obscured. Nutrition education too was dislodged from its ecological and cultural moorings and concentrated instead on 'selling' nutritional disorders and their cures.

Nutrition scientists talked of the high incidence of protein deficiency among people and advocated the use of animal protein, thus creating a market for the protein food industry. The same was true for body foods. In fact, so pervasive was the influence of these market forces on nutrition research and practice, that nutritionists came to be looked upon as 'sales agents' of these industries. But it is undoubtedly true that their preoccupation with research has taken them far away from the ecological, sociological, economic and political factors that impinge upon the nutritional status of a people. In the words of J. Gussow (1981) :

Fearing that we would not be taken seriously as scientists... we have attended to the ever smaller and smaller...breaking down food, food handling, food processing, food functions, into manageable microscopic pieces; looking at the isolated effects of the isolated biological systems. I believe it is time now for some of us in the field of food and nutrition to take up our microscopes to begin the task of looking at connections not merely between nutrients and cells or between food handling, food textures and food toxins, but of looking at the connections between farmers and producers; between food policies and environmental policies; between toxic wastes and the opportunity to produce safe affordable food.

Unless we imbibe this, unless we look at the problems from a holistic perspective, little can be done towards alleviating the problems of malnutrition.

Malnutrition and the Availability of Food

India has made considerable progress in foodgrain production, registering an increase from 50 million tonnes in 1950 to 152.37 million tonnes in 1983-84 and to about 170 million tonnes in 1988-89. The rate of food production has always exceeded the population growth rate of 2.5 per cent per annum. The data on per capita net availability of foodgrain reveals that in 1951 it was 394.9 gm per day, as compared to 465.5 gm per day in 1987. The per capita net availability of cereals during the same years was 334.2 and 429.3 gm, respectively. However, the per capita availability of pulses declined from 60.7 gm to 36.2 gm. In a country as vast as India, overall figures for food production provide a rather misleading picture of the actual situation as they tend to mask certain striking regional imbalances. The phenomenal success of the Green Revolution, for instance, is largely attributable to the performance of only two states — Punjab and Haryana. Per capita food production actually deteriorated in Madhya Pradesh, Maharashtra, Rajasthan, Tamil Nadu and Kerala.

Food production policies have also contributed to these imbalances. A case in point is the substitution of food crops with cash crops meant primarily for export. The cultivation of soyabean in Madhya Pradesh has replaced the cultivation of coarse grains which constitute the staple diet of the poor. In other areas, potato cultivation has been replaced with sugarcane which yields less calories per hectare than the former. The most unfortunate aspect of such policies — the adverse effect on nutrition besides — is that the benefit of export earnings do not reach the poor at all. Similarly, although the Green Revolution has resulted in a significant increase in the production of wheat and rice, it has had no impact on the production of pulses and legumes, which ensure the protein content in cereal-based diets, or on coarse grains and oilseeds. In fact, the prices of pulses and edible oils have increased to levels that make them inaccessible to lower income groups whose need for these is the most acute. Unfortunately, it is the nutritionally vulnerable groups which are least able to get coarse grains, cheap pulses and vegetable oils. We are thus faced with the cruel paradox of a Green Revolution that has augmented cereal production while indirectly contributing to an impairment of the nutritional status of poor households.

An analysis of National Sample Survey data on nutrition by P.G.K. Panikar revealed that in Karnataka, Gujarat and Maharashtra, over two-thirds of the diet of the rural population comprised of coarse cereals. The steep rise in the price of coarse grains resulted in a decline in the average intake of calories among the rural population. In Orissa, Assam, Bihar, Andhra Pradesh, West Bengal, Tamil Nadu and Kerala, rice constituted the principal component of the cereal basket — in 1961-62 it accounted for 83 per cent of the diet and declined to 78 per cent a decade later. The average intake of calories also declined during this period. The study concluded that the nutrition level in these states is precarious and their deficiency seems to be chronic. In the Green Revolution states of Punjab and Haryana too, the average intake of calories has shown a declining trend. This is because several poor peasants and labourers are denied the benefits of the Green Revolution. Access to technological inputs is usually denied to them and the surplus food is produced by the rich farmers who demand higher prices and subsidised inputs. Marginal farmers are often forced to sell part of their produce to the large farmers to repay loans they are forced to take in times of need. They sometimes buy back their produce, but at an enhanced price. Many have joined the ranks of landless labourers. This is not to deny the advantages of the Green

Revolution, but to point out the failure to build the necessary safeguards in the development process to prevent the deleterious repercussions on the weaker sections.

The public distribution system too has failed to reach the most deprived, both in the rural areas and in the urban slums. D. Banerji's study (1985) of nineteen villages reveals that about 35 per cent of the population does not get two square meals a day for more than three months in a year. Moreover, the proportion of poor in the population will increase sharply if the criterion of 'square meals' is replaced by 'wholesome meals' which includes a small quantity each of pulses, ghee/oil and iron in the case of adults, and the addition of milk in the case of children.

Related to the problem of food production is that of storage. Some amount of foodgrain is lost due to pest attacks, some during the post-harvest season, and some due to inefficient storage facilities which expose the grain to moisture, rats and fungi. Not only does this result in a considerable loss of available foodgrain, but points to the lag between technical knowledge and its application at the field level.

The faulty distribution system too contributes to extensive losses. Often surplus production of certain perishable foods results in a glut in the local market, while the same commodities are found to be scarce in other parts of the country. Thus, inadequate distribution facilities merely result in the crop being destroyed. The equitable distribution of available food would go a long way towards combating malnutrition. Unfortunately, however, the distribution is uneven not only between regions but within households as well. Hence, an increase in food production alone is not the answer, the solution lies in tacking the socio-economic factors that prevent people from getting what they need. In fact foodgrain stocks increased from 11.7 million tonnes in 1980 to 19.2 million in 1985. But the masses simply cannot afford to purchase it. What is this if not a situation of poverty in the midst of plenty? Should our buffer stocks not be seen as an indication of the level of poverty of the masses? Is it surprising then that malnourishment is a problem most acute among the poor and the underprivileged?

Nutritional Situation in India

The most glaring nutritional disorders in India are : (a) protein energy malnutrition (PEM), defined as a range of pathological conditions arising from a deficiency of proteins and calories. The two distinct clinical disorders associated with PEM are kwashiorkor and marasmus; and (b) disorders resulting from deficiencies of iron (iron deficiency anaemia), vitamin A (keratomalacia or nutritional blindness), iodine (goitre), and vitamin B (angular stomatis, gossitis).

Since 1972, the National Nutrition Monitoring Bureau (NNMB) of the Indian Council of Medical Research (ICMR) has been monitoring nutritional status in the states of Kerala, Andhra Pradesh, Karnataka, Maharashtra, Orissa, Gujarat, Tamil Nadu, Madhya Pradesh, Uttar Pradesh and West Bengal. From each state 500 rural and 250 urban households were selected for the study. The urban sample was further divided into five distinct socio-economic groups — high income group (HIG), middle labour and slum dwellers. Several extensive surveys on good consumption were also carried out by the food and Nutrition Board (FNB) and notwithstanding differences in coverage and sampling design, the NNMB and FNB data provide the most authentic sources of the nutritional status of the Indian population. The NNMB data revealed that in nearly half the households surveyed, diets were deficient even on the basis of the lowered yardstick of adequacy (m-2SD) of mean requirement.

Contrary to the general belief that iron deficiency anaemia is prevalent only among women in the reproductive age, several studies carried out under the auspices of the ICMR have shown it to be as much a problem of preschool children and even adult men. Another study by the NIN showed that 65 per cent of adult women, 75 per cent of pregnant women, 77 per cent of preschool children and 45 per cent of adult men in poor rural communities suffered from iron deficiency anaemia, making it the most extensive nutritional deficiency disorder in the country.

Keratomalacia, arising primarily from vitamin A deficiency, has been the major cause of nutritional blindness in children, particularly children between 1 and 3 years of age. Although there are no accurate estimates available of the prevalence of keratomalacia, rough estimates from hospital records reveal it to be a major problem. Field data too does not reveal the accurate picture because of the short duration of the disease itself and because a high percentage of those who turn blind as a result of keratomalacia die from neglect. The prevalence of Bitot's spots, a less serious manifestation of vitamin A deficiency in older children, is taken as a rough measure of the problem. The clinical manifestations of vitamin A deficiency reveal it to be a public health problem of considerable significance, and one that is closely associated with income levels.

Women and Nutritional Status

Although NNMB data does not reveal significant differences between the nutritional status of men and women, several micro studies have shown that the diets of female children and women are inadequate as a result of discrimination in intra-household food allocation. Discrimination against females begins during infancy. Starting with breast-feeding, infant girls receive less milk, less frequently and for shorter periods than boys. Where there is already one surviving child, it has been found that the girl child has a greater mortality risk. Weaned earlier, they do not get the required quantity of food, predisposing them to malnutrition. Studies have shown this problem to continue through childhood and adolescence. In times of food scarcity, women's access to food is further circumscribed. A survey of flood-hit villages in Bengal in 1978 showed a higher incidence of malnutrition among girls under 6 years. Micro-level studies of the nutritional status of adults of different socio-economic backgrounds also reveal significant male/female differences with poor women being the most deprived.

Females are also discriminated against in terms of the quality of food available to them. In Punjab, it was found that under 4 males receive larger quantities of cereals, fats, milk and total calories than females. A major consequence of such discrimination is that girls fail to achieve full growth potential NNMB (1980) data shows that between 12 and 33 per cent of women in the 20 to 24 age group have heights less than 145 cm and between 15 and 29 per cent have weights below 38 kg.

Below these levels women are at risk from obstetric complications and tend to produce low birth weight babies, thus furthering the vicious cycle. In a study, a 35.5 per cent incidence of low birth weight babies was found among poor, short women, while a 24 per cent incidence was found among poor women over 145 cm in height.

Several studies have been undertaken on the effects of low dietary intake and maternal malnutrition on pregnancies. The dietary intake of low income groups ranges from 1,200 to 1,600 calories per day. It has also been found that there is nc increase in this intake during pregnancy, with weights ranging between 40-45 kg with an increase during pregnancy of 6 kg. If there is : (a) an interval between pregnancies of at least two years, (b) no further reduction in dietary intake, and (c) no increase in physical activity, and any adverse effects on maternal nutrition and on pregnancies can be averted. In the event, such women give birth to children with birth weight between 2.5 to 3 kg and have shown themselves to be victims of malnutrition and anaemia. Furthermore, it is well-established that infections further impair the nutritional status of an individual by altering absorption and metabolism and through the excretion of nutrients in the case of diarrhoea and vomiting. There is evidence that prompt medical attention in the case of illness is often denied to females, thus adversely affecting their nutritional status.

❑❑❑

INDEX

A

Agricultural biodiversity, 20
Agricultural biodiversity, Conservation, 21
Agricultural Development, 7
Agricultural Globalization, 53
Agricultural Productivity, 4
Agro-Biodiversity Management, 138
Asia Pacific Region, Land use Pattern, 129
Asia, Pacific Region, Research Priorities, 138
Asia-Pacific Region, Crop Production, 129
Asia-Pacific Region, Plant Genotic Resources, 108

B

Biodiversity, Agricultural, 20
Biodiversity Benefits, 19
Biodiversity Conservation, 14, 162
Biodiversity Threats, 17
Biodiversity Benefits, Economic Benefits, 19
Ecological Services, 19
Cultural-anthropological, 19
Recreational and Aesthetic utility, 20
Biodiversity components, Spices diversity, 14; Genetic diversity, 15; Ecosystem diversity, 16
Biodiversity Threats, Natural extinction Threat, Human Activities, 17
Biological Heritage Protection, 84
Biological Piracy, 91
Biotechnology Development, 162

C

Chemicalisation, 25
Colorisation of Agriculture, 149
Cropping Systems, 154

D

Diversity Networks, 33
Drought, 219

E

East-Asia, Agriculture, 123
Ecology, Human, 1
Ecology, Technological Changes, 145
Economic Development, Appropriate Policies, 9
Economic Development, Small Farms, 46
Economic Globalization, Women, 28
Ecosystem Diversity, 16
Ecosystem Service, 47
Empowerment of Women Hinduism, 191
Empowerment of Women, 198

F

Feminism in India, 180
Feminism, Modern State, 186
Food Availability, Malnutrition India, Nutritional Situation, 225, 228
Food Insecurity, Globalization, 42
Food Production, Globalization, 43

G

Gender Issues, 172
Gender & Society, 172
Gender Studies, 172
Genetic Engineering, 24
Global Food System, 42
Globalization, Agriculture, 53
Globalization, Food Insecurity, 42
Globalization, Food Production, 43
Green Revolution, 2

H

Health & Healing, Indian Status, 219
Health Status, India, 219
Heritage Protection, Biological, 84
Intellectual, 84
Human Ecology Concept, 1

I

India's Health, Status, 219
Indian Status, Health & Healing, 219
Intellectual Heritage Protection, 84
Intellectual Piracy, 91
Intellectual Property and the Politics of Knowledge, 165

Intensive Tribal Development Agency, 70
IPR Regimes, 104

K

Knowledge System Exploration, 180
Knowledge System, Pluralism, 87
Knowledge Systems, Hierarchy, 88
Land Reforms, 47
Malnutrition Socio-cultural Factors, 222
Malnutrition, 219
Malnutrition, Food Availables, 225
Malnutrition, Poverty, 221
Malnutrition, Socio-Cultural Factors, 221

N

Natural Forest Ecosystem, 114
Nutrition Situation, India, 228
Nutrition Status, 219
Nutritional Status, Women, 229

P

Pacific Island Countries, Agriculture, 125
Patent Regimes, Western, 100
Piracy, Biological, 91
Piracy, Intellectual, 91
Plant Genetic Resources, Asia-Pacific Region, 108
Plant Genetic Resources, Conservation, 108
Plant Genetic Resources, Utilization, 108
Pluralism, Knowledge System, 87
Poverty, Malnutrition, 221
Private Sector Campaigns, 71
Productivity, Small Farms, 45
Public Sector, 55
    Campaigns, 69
    Privatisation, 57
    Structure, 58
    World Bank Funding, 61

S

Scheduled Caste Women and Changing Trends, 207
Seed Corporation, 59
Seed Policy, 56
Small Farms Productivity, 45
Small Farms, Economic Development, 46
Socio-cultural Factors, Malnutrition, 222
Sorghum Market, 78
South-Asia, Plant Genetic Resources, 112
South-East Asia, Agriculture, 117
Spinning Wheel, tool for development, 149
Sustainable Agricultural Development, 7
Sustainable Agriculture, 4
Sustainable Agriculturing, 14
Sustainable Agriculture, Threats, 24

T

Technological Changes, Ecology, 145
Textile Industry, Technology innovation, 149
Toxic Diversity, 15
TRIPS Agreement, 97

V

Varna theory, 183
Vegetable Market, 79

W

Woman Experiment, Structural Transferments, 199
Woman, Food security networks, 34
Women Empowerment, 198
Women Empowerment, Holishi Approach, 200
Women Hinduism Empowerment, 19
Women Networks, 36
Women States, Development Experiment, 196
Women, Biodiversity Networks, 35
Women, Cultural Diversity Networks, 38
Women, Economic Diversity Networks, 37
Women, Economic Globalization, 28
Women, Health Networks, 36
Women, Intellectual Property Rights, 36
Women, Nutritional Status, 229
Women's Lives, Religious Ideology, 193
Women's Studies, 173
    Gender issue, 172
    Models, 176